MUHAMMEDAN LAW

OF

MARRIAGE AND DIVORCE

COLUMBIA UNIVERSITY PRESS
SALES AGENTS

NEW YORK
LEMCKE & BUECHNER
30-32 WEST 27TH STREET

LONDON
HUMPHREY MILFORD
AMEN CORNER, E.C.

CONTRIBUTIONS TO ORIENTAL HISTORY AND PHILOLOGY

NO. VII

MUHAMMEDAN LAW
OF
MARRIAGEAND DIVORCE

BY

AHMED SHUKRI, LL.B., M.A.

SUBMITTED IN PARTIAL FULFILMENT OF THE REQUIREMENTS FOR THE DEGREE OF DOCTOR OF PHILOSOPHY, IN THE FACULTY OF POLITICAL SCIENCE, COLUMBIA UNIVERSITY

New York
COLUMBIA UNIVERSITY PRESS
1917

NOTE

It is a happy augury of our enlarged point of view that we are beginning to try to understand those from whom we differ. This is true especially of Turkey and, in general, of all Muhammedan countries. We, therefore, welcome the study presented here of the Muhammedan laws and customs relating to marriage and divorce. Though not unaffected entirely by earlier and foreign systems of jurisprudence, this portion of Muhammedan law has remained comparatively unaffected by modern European legislation. It has stood as the private concern of Muhammedan states and communities; and we are enabled to obtain here a view of the social development of Islamic society which is either denied us in other fields or is rendered more complicated by diverse influences from the outside. A study like the following has, therefore, a value above and beyond the confines of pure law. Dr. Shukri has not confined himself to one branch of Muhammedan legal law, but has embraced in his presentation the points of view of the chief schools that have had a part in its development.

RICHARD GOTTHEIL

CONTENTS

INTRODUCTION

MUHAMMEDAN JURISPRUDENCE

Sources of the Law and Methods of Interpretation

The development of Muhammedan jurisprudence began after the death of Muhammed. Prior to his death, the Arabian Prophet ruled absolutely. Any decision of his was valid; his dicta in all matters of religion and law were inspired by God; most of his decisions were God's, both in language and in thought. He had no need of a code; his declaration of the law was enough. From the point of view of Muhammed, respect for authority was the pillar of the law. "Obey God and his Apostle, that ye may obtain mercy" is the canon upon which his whole system rests.

So long as Muhammed lived, the faithful were in possession of a door communicating, so to speak, with the throne of God. All they had to do was to knock at this door, state their perplexities, and a response came to them from the "Lord of the Glorious Throne" which settled the difficulty once for all. After the death of the Prophet, 632 A. D., when the spiritual and wordly government of the Muhammedan commonwealth devolved on his companions, who enjoyed no such authority, the people were deprived of the most effective means of settling their difficulties. But this was not the only means. When Muhammed found his end approaching, he addressed the assembled Muslims from Mount Arafat, and explained to them where they were to find precepts for their guidance: "Oh people! Listen to my words, as I may not be another year with you in this place. Be humane and just among yourselves... Fix my words in your memory well. I have revealed to you everything; I have left to you a law which you should preserve and be firmly attached to—a law clear and positive, the Book of God and the conduct of His Prophet." "The Book" which Muhammed bequeathed to his people was the collection of those revelations which were made to him when he was vested with the office of the Prophet and Messenger of God. According to Orthodox Muhammedans, its text existed from eternity and was communicated to the Prophet from time to time in verses.

Since the Muhammedan community was to be governed largely by these revelations, the necessity of collecting and putting these verses into written form forced itself upon the attention of the early Muslims.[1] During the life of Muhammed the texts of the Koran had been preserved in the memories of his companions, inscribed on bones, date leaves and tablets of stone. The result of the codification was not only a compendium of religious dogma, but a code of rules regulating civil, criminal, political, administrative and economical matters, covering the whole domain of the private and public life of the citizen.

That a work so comprehensive in character should have been found, soon after Muhammed's death, to be incapable of meeting all the varying conditions of the social life of a rapidly growing community, and that supplementary sources of law should be found necessary, was only natural. Muhammed himself, with characteristic insight, foresaw this. A tradition asserts that, when he sent Mu'adh ibn Jebal to Yemen as governor, he asked him what would be his guiding principle in deciding cases. Mu'adh replied: "The Book

[1] For the history and codification of the Koran see: The Sacred Books of the East; vol. VI.

of God." "But suppose you find nothing applicable to the case before you?" inquired the Prophet. "Then the rulings and traditions of His Prophet" (*sunnah*). "And if that does not suffice?" asked Muhammed. "Then by deduction, after the best of my judgment" (*ijtihad*) . . . Muhammed thereupon is said to have lifted up his eyes to heaven and thanked God for having raised up men so capable of serving the true interests of religion.

In this accepted tradition we have the high authority of Muhammed for the principles on which from the outset Muhammedan jurisprudence was based. The process of applying these principles was a practical one. To decide cases, the jurists had first "The Book"—the Koran. If no provision covering the case was found in the Koran, they had recourse to the precepts and usage of the Prophet: *i. e.* what he said and did as judge, as theologian, or simply as a man in the ordinary events and vicissitudes of life. If a rule were still lacking, there was the customary law of Medina and the agreement of the Muslim people. Lastly there were analogy and common sense, or equity. With these was built up an elaborate structure, forming a complete guide to a man's duty under all contingencies, to God, to other men, and to himself, and necessarily including what we should today call systems of civil and criminal law. The people of Muhammed, in the contemplation of the first jurists, was to be an elaborate unity. State and Church, theology and law, conduct and morals, were to be but phases of the life of an undivided organism. As Muhammed had been ruler, judge, creed-maker and pattern for his people, that people was to be all this for itself in the centuries to come.

With the wide sweep of Muslim conquest, however, another source of law became active. This was Roman law, which the Muhammedan jurists found in use in the conquered Roman provinces. It is true that Muhammedan law rests completely upon the revelation and the conduct of the Prophet, and that the jurists have to deduce their rules from these sources; but Roman law seems nevertheless to have become an indirect source, in that it helped them draw their analogies (*qias*).

It must be remembered that the Arab armies were not devastating hordes; they recognized the need of law and order wherever they went, and it was their policy to take over the administrative system of the countries which they occupied. It is probable that the intercourse of the Arabs with Syrian Christians, who played a prominent part at the Omeyyad court at Damascus, introduced them to the theories of the Roman law; for when the province passed under the rule of the Arabs, the law books of Justinian and their use survived the Muslim conquest.[1]

As the Teutonic barbarians in their conquest of the western Roman provinces left the Roman law intact in so far as the Romans were concerned, so did the Arabs permit their non-Musulman subjects to administer justice between themselves according to their own laws.[2] During the administration of the Khalif Muawiyah at Damascus the Roman administration of law remained undisturbed. The magistrate rendered the formula and the judex tried cases according to the instructions contained in the formula.[3] This system lasted for a whole century.[4]

The Abbasides loved and patronized learning and extended special encouragement to the jurists. Baghdad, their capital, became the centre of culture and attracted

[1] A. von Kremer, Kultur-Geschichte des Orients unter den Kalifen; vol. I., p. 534. According to von Kremer even Arabia was acquainted with the Roman law, particularly through the Jews, whose laws were influenced by those of Rome. See: p. 535.

[2] Thus the Moors after their conquest of Spain left the local laws untouched. Lurent, Histoire de Droit des Gens, vol. V., p. 468 citing: Fauniè; Histoire de la Gaule Meridionale, Vol. III, p. 52.

[3] Savvas pasha, Etude sur la Theorie Musulman, p. 57.

[4] Ibid. p. 95.

jurists from Syria, Mesopotamia and the East-Roman Empire. The study of Greek and Roman literatures and sciences also came into considerable vogue about this time. Students of comparative jurisprudence cannot fail to note the similarity between many parts of Muhammedan and Roman jurisprudence. The Arabic legal nomenclature in some instances shows signs of literal translation from Latin, and there are various maxims of the Muhammedan law which suggest a Roman origin. What is perhaps most important, Muhammedan legal interpretation seems to have been influenced by the freedom with which this method of legal development had been used by the Roman jurists in their *responsa* and by their recognition of natural law as "a legal reservoir". In its earliest stages, Muhammedan law accorded to the judge a liberty of opinion which went beyond even that of the *responsa prudentium* and anticipated English equity.

There is, however, another side to the question. Comparative jurisprudence is a fascinating subject; similarities between two systems may easily be over-emphasized; and there is a temptation to assume derivation whenever there is correspondence. It is quite possible that a similitude which strikes us as remarkable may after all be simply the product of minds fashioned in legal modes of thought, pursuing similar paths of inquiry and arriving independently at identical principles. The Roman law was the expression of the highest reason among a cultured people having a peculiar talent for administration, and it is not so extraordinary as to render it impossible that a race like the Saracens, also possessing great administrative genius, and highly intelligent, should work out for themselves general principles of law which coincide with those propounded by Roman jurists.[1] In some instances, however, the similarity between Roman and Muhammedan rules and principles

[1] W. H. Rattigan, 17 Law Quarterly Review, p. 413.

seems too close to be dismissed as mere coincidence.[1] The question is one which invites closer and more extended investigation than it has yet received, before any definite opinion can be expressed upon it.[2]

Schools of Jurisprudence

The attitude of Muhammed towards the study and practice of law was most favorable. In at least two well known traditions he declares: "If God favors one of his creatures, He gets him to study the law and makes him a lawyer"; and: "A lawyer is proof against the devil, who tampers with the ignorant in the prayer." It is not surprising, therefore, to find among the Muhammedans, from the very outset, men who equalled the jurists of any age, with the possible exception of the immortal Roman *jurisprudentes.*

The struggles of these jurists to adapt the original simple material, largely casuistic, to varying conditions, climates and times has, as might have been expected, led to the formation of several legal schools, some of which survive to this day.

A schism, dating back to the martyrdom of the great Khalif Ali, has divided the Muslim world into two great sects: *Sunnites* and *Shi'ites.* The differences between the *Sunnis* and the *Shias* center rather in questions relating to political events of the past than in principles of law or jurisprudence. The present study deals exclusively with the *Sunnite* jurists. Among them two divergent tendencies were manifested from the outset, represented respectively by "the followers of private judgment and analogy, who were natives of Irak, and the followers of tradition,

[1] Seignette, Code de Khalif, p. 37.

[2] There is an interesting essay by Prof. Evaristo Carusi entitled: Sui rapporti fra diritto romano a diritto musulmano. Atti della Società Itl. per il progresso delle Scienze, 1913.

who were natives of Hijaz. As the people of Irak possessed but few traditions, they had frequent great recourse to analogical deductions and attained great proficiency therein, for which reason they were called the followers of private judgment. Their chief was the Imam Abu Hanifa. The people of Hijaz had for their leaders first Malik and then Shafi'i".[1]

Hanifites.

Abu Hanifa Numan Ibn Thabit was born at Kufa in Irak, 699 A. D., and died in 767. He was not an Arab, but belonged to a noble Persian family. Ibn Khallikan characterizes him as "a learned man, a practiser of good works, remarkable for self-denial, piety, devotion and the fear of God, humble in spirit, and constant in his acts of submission to the Almighty." It is related that he was a man of so retiring a disposition that he suffered stripes and imprisonment rather than undertake the office of a judge. Al-Mansur, the Khalif, had him brought from Kufa to Baghdad in order to appoint him as judge, but Abu Hanifa refused to act. "Al-Mansur then swore that he should act; the other swore that he would not; the Khalif repeated his oath, and so did Abu Hanifa. On this the chamberlain, Ar-Rahi Ibn Yunus, said to him: 'Do you not perceive that the Commander of the Faithful has made an oath?' Abu Hanifa replied: 'The Commander of the Faithful has ampler means than I for expiating an oath not fulfilled.' As he persisted in refusing, the Khalif sent him to prison,"[2] and on another occasion Yazid ibn Omar inflicted on him "one hundred and ten strokes of a whip; ten every day"[3] for the same cause.

Abu Hanifa was a highly religious man. It is said that he spent his nights in reciting the Koran, and his sobbings

[1] Ibn Khaldun, Prolegomena to Universal History, pp. 372, 373.
[2] Ibn Khallikan's Biographical Dictionary.
[3] Ibid.

were so loud that the neighbors would pray God to have pity on him. In the place where he died, it is said, he had recited the entire Koran seven thousand times. That a man of such a disposition should refuse the office of judge is not surprising. There are numerous traditions that set forth the responsibilities incurred by the Muslim who assumes the position of a judge or a divider between his fellow-men, and the terrible penalties awaiting the judge who deviates from the straight path of equity. One of the traditions says: "He who shall be appointed judge over men is verily slain with a knife; and on the day of resurrection there will come, even upon a just judge, such fear and horror that he will wish: 'Would to God I had not ordered between two persons in a trial even on a single occasion.' For there is no judge who orders between men, whether he be just or unjust, but will come to God's court on the day of resurrection held by the neck by an angel; and the angel will raise his head up toward the heavens and wait for God's orders to throw him into hell; the angel will do it from a height of forty days' journey"

Abu Hanifa had studied jurisprudence under Hammad ibn Ali Suleiman (*ob. circa* 737). From this master he learned the application of analogy (*qias*) which continued to be the rule of his school. To him, as to many other Muhammedans, the work of his life was revealed through a dream. He dreamed that he was digging open the tomb of the Prophet; and when he sought for an interpretation, he was informed that he would lay open a science never before disclosed.

He achieved an immense fame by reason of his knowledge of the law, and the subtlety and acuteness he displayed in its interpretation. Malik is reported to have said of him that he was a man of such talent that if he undertook to demonstrate that pillars were made of gold he could do so.

His system of jurisprudence is distinguished from the others by the length to which he carried the process of analogical deduction. An example of this is the extension he gave to the rule in the Koran prohibiting winedrinking. A beverage of an intoxicating nature called *arak*, not being known in the time of Muhammed, was not mentioned; but it was decided by reasoning from analogy that the drinking of this particular beverage should also be included among things prohibited.[1] In like manner the contract of hiring and letting was unknown but Abu Hanifa introduced it as analogous to contract of sale and purchase.[2]

The body of doctrine passing under his name was elaborated in part only by Abu Hanifa; in even larger measure it proceeded from his two disciples, the Imam Abu Yusuf, consulting lawyer of Khalif Harun Al Rashid, and the Imam Abu Muhammed, both of whom almost overshadowed their master. Hanifa's teaching was oral, and it was by his disciples that his doctrines were incorporated in formal treatises. Owing to their being adopted by the Abbaside Khalifs of Baghdad, and later by the Ottoman Khalifs, the Hanifite doctrines, which before had chiefly prevailed in Persia among the Turkish tribes, have become those officially recognized in the Ottoman Empire. They are the prevailing doctrines in Egypt, Arabia and India and have by far the greatest number of adherents.

Malikites.

The founder of the school commonly known as that of the Malikites was Malik ibn Anas (713-795 A. D.). He was a native and the judge (*kazi*) of Medina. The pious affection of his disciples has preserved many interesting personal traits of this celebrated jurist. He was, we are told of a very fair complexion, inclining to red. He was

[1] Savvas Pasha, Etude sur la theorie du Droit Musulman, p. 42.
[2] Ibid. p. 111.

tall in stature, having a large head, and the forehead bald. He wore clothes of the excellent stuffs imported from Aden. He disapproved of shaving off the moustaches, considering this to be a sort of mutilation; and he never changed the color of his hair by dyeing it.[1]

Like the Imam-al-A'zam (Abu Hanifa) he was an exceedingly pious man. When he was about to deliver traditions of the Prophet, he made an ablution, then seated himself in the middle of his mattress, and, spreading out his beard assumed a grave and dignified deportment. When asked his motive in making these preparations, he replied: "I delight in testifying my profound respect for the sayings of the Apostle of God, and I never repeat one unless I feel myself in a state of perfect purity." In accordance with the same spirit of veneration, it is said, he never went about on horseback in Medina, even when enfeebled by advancing years. "No", he would say, "I shall never ride in the city wherein the corpse of God's Apostle lies interred."

His followers and those who accepted other doctrines are unanimous in declaring that Malik was better acquainted with the Koran and the traditions of the Prophet than any other of the great Imams. Ibn Khallikan says Shafi'i, a student of Malik, related the following conversation between himself and Muhammed, the disciple of Hanifa: "Muhammed said to me: 'Which of the two is more learned, our master or yours?' meaning Abu Hanifa and Malik. 'Dost thou wish', said I, 'that I should answer with impartiality?' He replied that he did; and said: 'I then ask thee before God, which of the two is the more learned in the Koran, our master or yours?' 'Yours to a certainty', said he. 'I again ask thee seriously,' said I, 'which of the two is the more learned in the traditions (*sunna*), our master or your?' 'Yours, to certainty', he replied. 'I shall again

[1] **Ibn Khallikan's Biographically Dictionary.**

ask thee', said I, 'which of the two is the best acquainted with the sayings (sentences forming legal decisions) pronounced by the companions of God's Apostle; our master or yours?' 'Why, yours to a certainty', was the answer. 'Then', said I, 'there remain only the analogical deductions (*qias*); and if they be not drawn from the three sources we have just mentioned, from whence can they be drawn?' "

It would not be correct, however, to assume that Abu Hanifa lacked a sufficient knowledge of the traditions, or that he did not regard them as a legitimate source of law. Ibn Khaldun, the great Moorish historian, himself a Malikite, says: "Some prejudiced men say that some of the Imams had a scanty knowledge of the traditions, and that is the reason why they have reported so few of them. This cannot be true regarding the great Imams, because the law is based on the Koran and the traditions, and it was a duty incumbent upon them to seek out the traditions. But some among them accepted only a small number of traditions, because of the severity of the tests which they applied."[1]

Malik is regarded as a very high authority in the traditions (*hadith*), and his school is of a rigid traditionalism. He attached a preponderating weight to the usages and customs of Medina, relying on the presumption that they must have been transmitted from the time of the Prophet. The differences of opinion between Abu Hanifa and Malik are a consequence of the difference in their environment. Imam Malik was an Arab of the Arabs, and was born and brought up in a city filled with memories of the Prophet. He was a member of a society whose needs Muhammed had had especially in view in all his decisions. He was a practical man, having filled the position of a judge. Abu Hanifa, on the other hand, was not only of Persian descent, but lived in a city which had not been founded till after the death of the Prophet. It was a great centre of commerce, and a meeting

[1] Ibn Khaldun, Prolegomena to Universal History, p. 371.

place for men of diverse types and various habits and modes of life. He was rather a student than a man of affairs; a speculative or philosophical jurist, whose system was not based so much upon the exigencies of life and the teachings of experience as upon casuistry. It is not surprising, therefore, that the "quick-brained vagabond", a stranger to the country of the Prophet, should have little interest in traditions and should differ from the aristocrat of aristocrats, Malik, sitting in state, in the judgment seat at Medina. He differed from Malik in that he made almost no use of traditions as a source of law, admitting but a few of these as authorities for his system.

Malik, on the other hand, is said to be the first jurist who made a collection of "true traditions" which he called the beaten path" (*muwatta*). His collection was so called because it was founded on what he called the customs of Medina, and contained those acts, commands and prohibitions which were found in the Koran or had been sanctioned by the example or recognition of the Prophet. It was, in other words, the "beaten path" which the faithful had trodden, and along which it behooved true believers to walk in the future.

The doctrine of this school prevailed among the Moors of Spain and still counts numerous followers in Northern Africa. Had it not been for the Turkish invasion of Egypt, it might have prevailed there over the Hanifite doctrine.

Shafi'ites.

The founder of the third orthodox school of jurisprudence was the Imam Abu Abdullah Muhammed ibn Idris Al-Shafi i. He was born in Palestine in 767 A. D., on the very day, it is said, on which Hanifa died. He was descended from Abd-al Muttalib, the grandfather of the Prophet. "Shafi'i stood unrivaled by his abundant merits and illustrious qualities; to the knowledge of all the sciences connected with the 'Book of God' and the traditions, the sayings of the companions, their history, the conflicting opinions of the learned, *etc.*, he united a deep acquaintance with the language of the Arabs of the desert, philology, grammar and poetry; indeed, he was so well acquainted with the latter that Al-Asma'i, eminent as he was in these branches of learning, read over the poems of Hudalites under his tuition. He combined in himself such a variety of scientific information as was never possessed by any other man; and Ahmed ibn Hanbal went so far as to say: 'I did not know the annulling from the annulled traditions, till I took lessons from Shafi'i!' "[1] Abdullah, the son of Hanbal, according to the same authority, asked his father what sort of a man Shafi i was. Hanbal is said to have answered: "My dear boy, Shafi'i was to mankind as the sun is to the world, and health to the body; what can replace him?"

The great work which Shafi'i was destined to do was, as usual, revealed in a dream. Before he was born, his mother dreamed that the planet Jupiter came forth from its place and proceeded to Egypt, where it fell, but that a portion of its rays reached every city upon the earth. The interpreters of dreams declared this to signify that she would give birth to a learned man, who would communicate his knowledge to the people of Egypt alone, but that it would spread to all other countries.

Shafi'i passed his youth at Mecca, where he learned by heart the Koran and "The Beaten Path" of Malik. He then went to take lessons from Malik, who told him to go to some person who would repeat to him "The Beaten Path." Shafi'i said that he already had a perfect knowledge of it, and recited it. Delighted with this mark of youthful zeal, the venerable Imam is reported to have said: "If any person is ever to prosper, it is this youth."

[1] Khallikan's Biographical Dictionary.

Shafi'i then went to Baghdad, but the greater part of his life was spent in Cairo, and there he is buried. Shafi'i is undoubtedly a prominent figure in the history of law. He does not seem to have possessed the originality and acuteness of Hanifa, but he was noted for his balance of judgment and moderation of views. Like Malik, he had a great reverence for tradition. "If you find a tradition from the Prophet saying one thing", he is said to have declared, "and a decision from me saying another thing, follow the tradition". Nevertheless, he examined the traditions more critically than did Malik; and he also allowed a greater scope to the consensus of opinion (*ijma'*), laying much stress on a tradition of the Prophet: "My people will never agree in an error."

The school of jurisprudence with which his name is associated takes rank, in the number and importance of its followers, next only to that of the Hanifites. The chief centre of his system was Egypt; followers of his school are found chiefly in parts of Africa, in Arabia, in India, and in Malay Archipelago.

Hanbalites.

Ahmed ibn Hanbal (781-855) was the founder of the fourth and last of the orthodox schools of jurisprudence. Like all traditionists of his period, he travelled in Syria, Mesopotamia, and in the Arabian peninsula, where he made some stay. He returned to Baghdad, where he sat at the feet of Shafi'i. He was a favorite pupil of Shafi'i, and when the latter went to Egypt he said: "I went forth from Baghdad, but left not behind me a more pious man or a better jurisconsult than Ahmed Hanbal."

Ibn Hanbal was rather a traditionist and theologian than a jurist. In the number of traditions stored up in his memory no one, even at that age, approached him. It is doubtful whether he ever had the intention of forming a school; least of all in opposition to his master Shafi'i. But being a pious man, he could not endure the evils which resulted from the abusive extension of the doctrine of analogy to its utmost limits. Baghdad was then at the height of its glory. In literature and in science it divided the supremacy of the world with Cordova; in commerce and wealth it far surpassed any city. How its splendor impressed the imagination may be seen from the stories of the *Arabian Nights*. The Khalifs lived in the midst of a luxury which has since come to be proverbial. Their palaces, and those of the nobles, blazed with gold and silver, and rang with the laughter of singing girls and the harmonies of musical instruments—harmonies profane to the pious Muslim. The court jurists were of Abu Hanifa's school. Many of them were notorious for their open and shameless application of the elastic rules of analogy to justify the most wanton excesses of arbitrary power and to pander to the licentious passions of Khalifs and governors. Ibn Hanbal's course was determined by the revolt of a clean heart and a clear conscience. He totally refused to accept the personal elucidation of any lawyer: he would admit no basis for the law save the Koran and the traditions of the Prophet. His attitude, however, was not in harmony with the spirit of his time. Mamoun at that time ruled at Baghdad, and the authority of revelation was subordinated to the higher law of reason. Greek philosophy was widely read, and the logic of Aristotle was fearlessly applied to shape the theology of the Koran into a system harmonizing with western ethics [1] Ibn Hanbal was persecuted and subjected to torture.[2]

[1] It may be interesting here to note that Greek philosophy was communicated to medieval Europe through Arab scholars and Muhammedan commentators, especially Avicenna (Ibn Sina) and Averroes (Ibn Rushd) of Cordova. The former is said to have read the Metaphysics of Aristotle forty times, until the very words were imprinted on his memory. See Renan, Averroes et l'averroisme; Madonnet. P., Siger de Bradant et, l'avverroisme latin au me siècle, 2nd Ed. 1911: F. Wuestenfeld, Geschichte der arabi-

He is said tc have withstood patiently both corporal punishment and imprisonment, without showing any willingness to modify his stubborn adherence to traditionalism.

His teaching made few proselytes beyond the province in which they were set forth. Here, however, the renown of his learning, piety and unswerving faithfulness to tradition gathered a host of disciples and admirers around him; and on his death, it is said, 800,000 men and 60,000 women attended his funeral and 20,000 Jews, Christians and fire-worshippers were converted to Muhammedanism.[1] Until the establishment of Turkish predominance in Islam, the Hanbalites, like the other three schools, were officially represented by a *Kazi* in every important Islamic centre. The predominance of the Ottoman Khalifs, however, dealt a severe blow to the Hanbalite school, which has since more and more dwindled away. In Damascus and other centers it has still a few adherents, who are distinguished for their fanaticism.

The Closed Door.

Like its conquests and its rapid growth in political power, the development of Islam's jurisprudence was spectacular. As an Empire was built upon the foundation of a few tribes, similarly a highly complex and refined system of jurisprudence was developed, within a few generations, out of a few barbarous tribal customs. Its growth and development was perhaps too rapid. Muhammedan lawyers contend that the "door of legislative effort" closed with the death of Ahmed Hanbal. To accept this notion, however, —to concede that the exposition of the law by the application of private judgment has ceased to be effective since

schen Aertzte und Naturforscher; G. Stockl, Philosophie des Mittelalters; T. J. de Baer, History of Philosophy in Islam.

[2] Abu Yahya Al-Nawawi, pp. 142, 143.

[1] Khallikan's Biographical Dictionary. But compare, Subki, Tabakat, vol. I., pp. 200, 201.

the third century of the Islamic era—would be to condemn Islam to a state of immobility, and to deprive its followers of the only means of adapting its doctrines to the everchanging necessities of time and place. Such a doctrine is contrary to the spirit of the Prophet's legislation, for a saying attributed to Muhammed declares that the rules of law change to suit the exigencies of the times. It is mainly through the operation of the power of interpretation that Muhammedan jurists have succeeded in developing the principles of their law into an intelligent system. No Muhammedan judge, worthy of the name, could refuse to decide a case on the ground that he could find in the sacred law no direct authority to guide him.

Savvas Pasha[1] thinks that it was the legends attached to Al-Gazali and Sadr-al-Shari'a Abdullah ibn Masud-ul-Mahbubi that gave rise to the notion that the door of "legislative effort" was closed. Both Gazali and Sadr-al-shari'a were filled with ambition to found a fifth school, but were prevented from doing so by divine intervention. It is said that Sadr-al-Shari'a, in a dream, found himself in a square mosque, having four doors and four windows above them. An angel approached him and asked him to introduce a fifth door without injuring the symmetry of the building. The jurist was embarrassed and was compelled to admit his incapacity to suggest a solution of the difficulty. The angel commanded him to reflect that the realization of his own design to become the founder of a fifth school would derange the whole fabric of Islam. The learned doctor accepted the lesson, renounced his ambitious project and pronounced the door of legislative effort to be henceforth closed for ever. Gazali, on the other hand, was prevented from founding a new school by the weighty consideration that the creation of a such school involving new theories and new methods, would be detri-

[1] Etude sur la theorie du droit Musulman, p. 142.

mental to the unity of Islam and to orthodoxy. However noble and sincere the motive might have been, it certainly was detrimental to the development of the law. The closing of the "door of legislative effort" meant the abandonment of inquiry concerning the spirit of the law. Discussion turned henceforth to the letter of the law; the questions debated were petty, involving the definition of terms, playing with words and scholastic refinements. It was not until a few months ago, with the wave of enthusiasm for reform in the Ottoman Empire, that it was declared that the door of legislative effort had never been closed.

Problems of Presentation

In endeavoring to set any part of the Muhammedan law in a foreign language, a writer encounters no slight difficulty. He finds no precise equivalents for technical terms, and, what is more serious, he finds in the foreign law nothing corresponding to the Muhammedan classification: similar topics are subsumed under different categories. In dealing with the latter problem, two courses were open: (1) to follow the arrangement of the Muhammedan jurists, or (2) to set forth the positive rules in arrangement more nearly corresponding to that employed in western systems of jurisprudence. Of these two methods the latter has been followed, in so far as it was found practicable. To follow the former method would plunge the western reader into a new world of concepts, with which he could only gradually familiarize himself, and would call upon him to think in a novel juristic atmosphere, in which he might at first fail to grasp the full meaning of what he read.

The translation of technical terms is always unsatisfactory. Each word has a history behind it, and to express all its connotations in one word in a foreign language is hardly possible. It is particularly difficult when the task is to express notions which prevailed in the ancient East in a language which prevails in the modern West. English, French and German translations have been consulted, and those terms which seemed most nearly adequate have been adopted. In many instances, however, new terms have been chosen or coined.

In reading this essay the reader is reminded that all the rules embodied therein are not necessarily in practice in states where the Muhammedan system of jurisprudence prevails. Some of these rules have been rendered obsolete by changes in the social structure and economic conditions. Such would be the case, for example, with provisions regarding slavery; this institution having been abolished in Turkey as in all other Muhammedan countries.

It remains for me gratefully to acknowledge the assistance I have received in my work from my esteemed professor, Munroe Smith, and to tender him my sincere thanks. He has shown me uniform kindness and courtesy, and has given me valuable advice and liberal assistance in my work. Had it not been for his inspiring suggestions this essay might never have been written. My thanks are also due to Professor Richard Gottheil for assistance with the proofs.

PART I

MARRIAGE

I. Legal View of Marriage

In modern law writings, generally, marriage is described as a contract—a contract by which a man and a woman reciprocally engage to live with each other during their joint lives, and to discharge toward each other the duties imposed by law upon husband and wife. Blackstone says: "Our law considers marriage in no other light than a civil contract."[1] This cannot seriously be argued. Marriage is essentially different from ordinary contracts in many respects. It differs in that it cannot be rescinded by either party or by both at pleasure. It creates, irrespective of the intentions of the parties, a status, in which their rights and duties are fixed by the law itself.

The Roman Catholic Church holds marriage to be a sacrament and, as such, indissoluble. Under Muhammedan law, marriage is one or the other or both. It is a contract, because it is based on mutual consent on the part of a man and a woman and is dissoluble almost at their option. It is a sacrament in so far as in this world it is an act of worship for it preserves mankind from pollution; it is an institution ordained for the protection of society, in order that human beings may guard themselves from unchastity. "The *Imams* are unanimous in recommending it to any person whose soul

[1] Commentaries, 1-432.

longs for it, and who is afraid of being tempted to commit fornication, in which case it will be more righteous to marry than to make a pilgrimage, or holy war, or optional prayers and fasting. He sins by omitting to do it, and by doing it he gets divine reward, if his intention is to protect himself from evil temptations, and to have children, when he is able to perform conjugal duties, and to pay the wife's dower and maintenance."[1]

The legal term for marriage is *nikah*. In its literal sense it means carnal union; in its legal sense it is described by the jurists as an agreement which results in the lawful enjoyment of woman, *mulk-al-muta*. *Muta* means enjoyment; *mulk* is used in different senses. One meaning is exclusive relationship; and in this sense it designates the special and devoted relationship between the wife and the husband. This interpretation has been ascribed to Shafi'i. The other meaning of mulk is ownership. Accordingly Mahmud Essad interprets the two words as meaning ownership of the right of enjoyment of the woman; not ownership of the person of the wife, or of anything not connected with the marital rights of the husband. This right of enjoyment is mutual. The reason why reference is commonly made only to the husband's right of enjoyment is because it belongs especially and pre-eminently to him. The wife is restricted to the enjoyment of her husband alone; the husband may legally marry other wives. The wife cannot claim intercourse with her husband as a matter of right, at least not more than once after marriage, while the husband is entitled to intercourse with his wife at his pleasure. The *Kifaya*[2] adds that the contract must have in view the procreation of children; for if enjoyment were the sole object or design of marriage, then a temporary marriage, which has nothing else in view, would be lawful.

[1] Abdul Kadir, Al-nahr; Durr-al-Muktar.
[2] Vol. II, p. 30.

Among the nations of antiquity polygamy seems to have been a recognized institution. "In the infancy of mankind, in early stages of society, when the cohesive power which serves in advanced periods to keep the different parts of the social fabric together is yet undeveloped, polygamy is a principle of race preservation. Man is the dominant element in these stages of the progress of humanity; woman is a mere subordinate. Her existence depended on her attaching herself to man, and the fact that women were more numerous than men gave rise to the custom which, in our advanced times, is rightly regarded as an unendurable evil."[1]

The moral purity of early peoples was of a kind altogether different from that which ascetic movements subsequently inculcated. Marriage was regarded almost exclusively as a gratification of the animal passions. The element of mutual attachment and respect between the contracting parties, the formation of household, and the entire complex of domestic feelings and family duties that have come to be associated with the household—all these had comparatively little recognition.

Polygamy was particularly prevalent among the oriental nations of antiquity, where it seems to have been necessitated by climatic and other circumstances.[2] It prevailed among Medes, Babylonians, Assyrians and Persians, without any restriction as to the number of wives; and among the Israelites, both before the time of Moses and after, the practice seems to have flourished.[3] It is true that monogamy is almost universally assumed to have prevailed in Greece, but what monogamy meant to the Greeks is indicated by the statement made by Demosthenes: "We have *heterai* for our pleasure, concubines for the ordinary requirements of the body, and wives for the procreation of lawful issue and as

[1] Seyid Amir Ali, Muhammedan Law, p. 217.
[2] Compare Montesquieu's Esprit des Lois, XVI—2—7.
[3] Exod. XXI 9 Lev. XVIII 18. Deut. XXXI 15-17.

confidential domestic guardians."[1]

Tacitus, who portrayed the purity of German life in the most flattering colors, did not conceal the fact that polygamy was practised by the nobility, and that a plurality of wives was looked upon as a badge of dignity.[2] Among the Franks "The Kings Caribet and Chilperic had both many wives at the same time.[3] Clothaire married the sister of his first wife during the lifetime of the latter. Theodebert, whose general goodness of character is warmly extolled by the episcopal historian, abandoned his first wife... took during her lifetime another and... upon the death of this second wife... took a third. St. Columbanus was expelled from Gaul chiefly on account of his denunciations of the polygamy of King Thierry.[4] Dagobert had three wives as well as a multitude of concubines. Charlemagne himself had at the same time two wives, and he indulged in concubines.[5]

"The greatest and most reprehensible mistake", says Amir Ali, "made by the Christian writers is to suppose that Muhammed either adopted or legalized polygamy." The Prophet found polygamy practised not only by his own people, but also among the people of the neighboring countries, where it assumed some of its most objectionable aspects. He simply accepted the system; he did not introduce it. This is the essential difference between Muhammedanism and Mormonism. Muhammed did not receive any revelation "on the eternity of the marriage convenant, or the plurality of wives." This honor belongs exclusively to the Mormon prophet Joseph Smith. Nor did the Arab Prophet

[1] Dem. C. Nocer. Att, v. 578; cf. Athen. XIII, 31. See also J. Dolinger, The Gentile and the Jew, vol. I p. 250; also A. W. Gellins, Noct. Att. XV, V. 20; Lecky, History of European Morals, vol. II, p. 295.

[2] Germania.

[3] Greg. Tur. IV, 26 and 28.

[4] Eginhardus, XXXVI.

[5] Lecky, History of European Morals, vol. II, p. 363. Charlemagne, according to Eginhardus had four wives. Vit. Kar. Mag. XVIII.

insist that his followers should take many wives. As a statesman he recognized polygamy as an ethnic condition, and he acted wisely in not interfering with it. Any radical innovation in this direction would have upset the entire fabric of Eastern society, and might have been fatal to Islam.

It is interesting to note that the sentence in the Koran which contains the permission to contract four contemporaneous marriages is immediately followed by an important qualification. The first passage says: "You may marry two, three, or four wives, but not more." The second reads: *"But if you cannot deal equitably and justly with all, you shall marry only one."*

In practice polygamy is fast disappearing. The institution was a product of earlier economic and social conditions and is dying away with the changing of the circumstances and the removal of the causes which produced it. "Harems", as represented to the Westerners are nothing but fantasies. If we leave out of account those Muhammedans who are still living under rather primitive conditions and those who, although nominally Muhammedans, are little influenced by ideals of law and religion or by healthy public opinion, monogamy is certainly the general rule and not the exception; while polygamy is regarded by the very few who practice it as a safeguard, however undesirable in itself, against greater social evils.

II. Impediments

The law imposes restrictions on the capacity of persons to marry certain other persons. These restrictions are in some cases perpetual and in others temporary.[1]

1. *Perpetual Impediments*

The perpetual prohibitions are based upon legitimate and

[1] Fetawa Kazi Khan.

illegitimate relationship of blood (consanguinity), affinity and fosterage.

a) Consanguinity.

By reason of consanguinity a man cannot marry any female ascendant or descendant of his, nor the daughter of any ascendant or descendant, nor the daughter of his brother or sister, nor the daughter of his brother's or sister's daughter, and so on.

This prohibition is based on the Koran, which says: "Ye are forbidden to marry your mothers, and your daughters and your sisters and your aunts, both on the father's and the mother's side; and your brother's daughters and your sister's daughters."[1] Bahr-ur-Raik sums up the prohibitions for men on grounds of consanguinity under the following heads:

(1) Mother and all female ascendants.

(2) Daughter and all female descendants.

(3) Sister and her female descendants.

(4) Brother's daughter and her female descendants.

(5) Father's sister (but not her daughter or any other descendant.)

(6) Mother's sister (but not her daughter or any other descendant.

Perceval, in his *Histoires des Arabes,* says that the pre-Muhammedan Arabs permitted the intermarriage of step-mothers and mothers-in-law on the one side with step-sons and sons-in-law on the other.[2] But the Koran expressly prohibits such unions. "Marry not women whom your fathers have had to wife, for this is an uncleanness, an abomination and evil way."[3] But a man may marry his father's wife's mother or daughter, unless fosterage create an impediment.[4]

[1] Koran, Sale's trans. vol. I, p. 92.
[2] Vol. I, p. 351.
[3] Ch. IV, v. 27.
[4] Khalil, Mukhtesar.

b.) *Affinity.*

On the ground of affinity a man is debarred from marrying:

(1) The mother of his wife and her grandmothers, whether on the father's or the mother's side.

(2) Daughters, granddaughters and great-granddaughters of the wife, provided always that the marriage from which this affinity results has been consummated. A retirement, which in many cases is equivalent to consummation, does not so operate in this case.

(3) The wife of a son or of a son's son or of a daughter's son. But it is not forbidden to marry the widow or divorced wife of an adopted son for such an agnatic (and purely artificial) relationship is not taken into consideration.

(4) The wives of fathers and grandfathers.

These prohibitions are included in the following passage from the Koran: "And your wives' mothers, and your step-daughters who are under your tuition, born of your wives unto whom you have gone in; but if you have not gone in unto them it shall be no sin to you to marry them; and the wives of your sons, who proceeded out of your loins."[1]

A man who has had illicit intercourse with a woman can marry neither her mother nor her daughter, and the woman herself is forbidden to his father and to his son. This is according to the Hanifites. Shafi'i maintains the contrary view, "because illicit intercourse does not induce prohibition from affinity, as this cause of prohibition is a peculiar distinction bestowed upon the servants of God through the divine favor, and fornication, being a crime, cannot possibly induce that which is a favor of God."[2] According to the Hanifites this prohibition is not only induced by fornication but also by lustful dalliance (*tactus*

[1] Ch. IV, v. 27.
[2] Hidaya.

immundus) or "by looking at the woman's nakedness with desire." This will not only establish a prohibition to marriage between each party and the ascendants or descendants of the other, but in case one of the parties is married to the ascendant or descendant of the other it will render further cohabitation unlawful.[1]

c.) *Fosterage.*

Generally speaking, fosterage produces the same impediments as affinity. Among the Hanifites, however, certain exceptions are made. A marriage between the father of the child and the mother or daughter of his child's foster-mother permissible. So also is a marriage between the foster-mother and the brother of the child whom she has fostered.

Among the Hanifites relation between fostermother and child, with the resulting impediments to marriage, is established when the child has been suckled once; but according to Shafi'ites it is necessary that it should have been suckled at least four times.[2]

2. *Temporary Impediments.*

The second class of impediments are of a temporary character.

a.) *Collateral affinity.*

It is forbidden to contract contemporaneous marriages with women so related to each other that, supposing either of them to be male, marriage between them would be illegal. "It is not lawful to marry and cohabit with two

[1] A female minor, being frightened in a dream flies towards father becomes disturbed (with desire) on seeing her, and she is eight years of age Sheikh-al-Iman Abu Kahir Muhammed, son her father's bed whilst she is in a state of nudity, and her become unlawful to her father.'" Kazi Khan.
of Fadal, on whom be peace, says: 'I fear her mother shall

[2] Khalil, Mukhtasar.

women being sisters... because the Almighty has declared that such cohabitation with sisters is unlawful."[1] If a man marries simultaneously and by one contract two sisters, or two women related to each other within the prohibitive degrees, both marriages are invalid, but if he marries them by two separate contracts, the first marriage is valid and only the second is illegal. If a man marries two sisters, one of whom he cannot lawfully marry (for example, by reason of her being the wife of another, or an idolatress, or for some other similar cause), the marriage is valid as regards the other sister, whom he might lawfully marry and it make no difference which of them he married first. This prohibition applies only to contemporaneous marriges. If a man wishes to marry one of two sisters after separating from the other, he is at liberty to do so.

b.) Iddah.

It is unlawful to marry the divorced wife or widow of another until the period of probation know as *iddah* has come to an end. This period is established "in order to know the cleanliness of the womb"; and the rules of *iddah* are based upon Almighty's saying: "And the divorced women should wait concerning themselves for three periods, *i. e.* until they have their courses thrice, and it shall not be lawful for them to conceal that which God has created in their wombs, if they believe in God and the last day."[2] This delay is provided in order to preserve pedigree and to save it from adulteration; *i. e.* in order to avoid uncertainty of paternity.

There is a difference of opinion between Abu Hanifa and Abu Muhammed on the one hand and Abu Yusuf on the other as to whether marriage may be contracted

[1] Hidaya, Bk. 2, ch. I.
[2] Koran, ch. II.

with a woman who is with child begotten out of wedlock Hanifa and his disciples hold that the marriage is lawful although the man must refrain from intercourse with the woman till her delivery. Abu Yusuf maintains that the union is illegal. Upon this point "our doctors (Hanifites) argue that the woman may lawfully be married on the authority of the sacred writings, the Koran saying: "All women are lawful to you, excepting those within the prohibited degrees'; and they say that the prohibition of cohabitation until after delivery is based solely on the impropriety of sowing seed in a soil already impregnated by another, a prohibition which occurs in the traditions. Abu Yusuf's allegation, that 'the illegality of the marriage in cases where the parentage of the fœtus is established originates purely in a principle of tenderness toward the fœtus' is altogether unfounded, for the nullity of the marriage in such a case originates in a regard for the right, not of the fœtus, but of the father." Malikites, Shafi'ites and Hanbalites are of the same opinion as Abu Yusuf. If a woman is pregnant by adultery with the man who marries her, the marriage is lawful and intercourse is not forbidden between them.[2]

Iddah, whether it follows divorce or widowhood, must be observed in the husband's home; and if the death of repudiation has occurred when the wife was away, she must return immediately, unless there is some valid reason why she cannot do so, *e. g.* because she will be liable for rent which she is unable to pay, or because the house can no longer be used for habitation.[3] *Iddah* is not incumbent on a wife repudiated before consummation of marriage.[4]

c.) Prior repudiation.

It is not lawful for a man to marry a woman whom he

[4] Koran, ch. XXXIII.
Musulman vol. I, p. 356.
[2] Rad-ul-Mukhtar, vol. II, p. 650 et seq. Also Clavel. Droit
[3] Rad-ul-Mukhtar, vol. II, p. 652.
[1] Hidaya.

has irrevocably repudiated unless she has subsequently become another man's wife. A woman is irrevocably repudiated if she has been divorced successively three times or if her husband divorces her by saying: "I have divorced you three times' or "let this be your third divorce." In these cases another marriage between the couple becomes illegal until after the consummation of a valid marriage to another man. This has led to a practice commonly known as *hullah,* which consists of employing a poor man or a blind man to marry the divorced woman and then promptly repudiated her.[1] Malik, however, holds that a woman irrevocably repudiated will not become free to marry her former husband by an intermediate marriage that is intended merely to legitimize her return.[2]

d.) Difference of religion.

Muhammed, in many instances, distinguished those whose religion is founded on the scriptures (*kitabis*), that is to say, Christians and Jews, from pagans; and so also in marriage, while it is forbidden to marry a polyt eistic woman, a marriage between a Christian or a Jewish wom n and a Muhammedan is perfectly valid. On the other hand, a marriage between a Muhammedan girl and a Christian or a Jew is illegal. The distinction is drawn between the case of a Muslim man and a Muslim woman because, if a Muslim woman were allowed to marry a Christian or a Jew, there would be a likelihood of her being converted to the faith of her husband, while in the opposite case there is deemed to be no cause for apprehension.

It is unlawful to marry a fire-worshipper (*Majusi*), God having said: "You may hold correspondence with the *majusis,* just as with the *kitabis,* but ye must not marry their daughters, nor partake of their sacrifices." Likewise

[1] For a detailed account of this institution see: Lane's Modern Egyptians.

[2] Khalil Mukhtasar.

it is unlawful to marry a pagan, the Koran having declared: "Marry not a woman of the polytheists until she embraces the faith." As to the Sabeans,[1] there is a difference of opinion between Abu Hanifa and his two disciples, Abu Yusuf and Abu Muhammed. The former contended that it was lawful to marry a Sabean woman, while his disciples maintained that the union was illegal. "The diversity of opinion which is recorded between Hanifa and his two disciples originates in their different ideas with respect to the Sabeans, each arguing from his own premises; for Hanifa accounts the Sabeans to be *kitabis* (believers in scriptures); whereas the two disciples consider them as worshippers of the stars.[2]

Malik, although tolerating marriage between Muhammedans and scriptural women, because of the express provision in the Koran, nevertheless regarded the practice with disfavor, especially in a non-Muslim country, "because a scriptural woman drinks wine, so contaminating her child even *in utero;* and her husband has no right to forbid her to drink or to prevent her going to church, *etc.* Malik regarded such marriages with greater abhorrence, because of the danger of the faith of the children of the marriage being corrupted.

With apostates, *i. e.* those who have forsaken the Muhammedan religion, marriage is always illegal.

e.) Pilgrimage

According to Shafi'ites, Malikites and Hanbalites, marriage during a pilgrimage to Mecca is prohibited. Hanifites, on the other hand, regard such a marriage as legal. The *Fetwa Alemkiri* expressly says it is lawful for a *muhrim* (a pilgrim) and a *muhrime* (fem.) to intermarry while in

[1] Haarbrucker, Religionspartheien etc. vol. II, p. 415.
[2] Hidaya.
[3] Khalil, Mukhtasar.

state of *ihram* (pilgrimage to Mecca). Shafi'i in support of his opinion quotes the Prophet as having declared: "*Muhrims* marry not, nor cause to marry."

The author of the *Hidaya* says: "in opposition to this our doctors (Hanifites) produce the instance of the Prophet himself who married Meymoona whilst he was a *Muhrim.*"

f.) Pentagamy.

As noted above it is not lawful to have more than four wives at the same time. According to Hanifites, the number of wives is further restricted in the case of slaves, who are not allowed more than two. Malik, however, maintains that slaves are capable of contracting four contemporaneous marriages. "The argument of our doctors (Hanifites) in this cases is, that slavery deprives a man of one-half of the natural privileges and enjoyments (of a free man), and the legal right to take four women in marriage being such a privilege, it follows that the right of a slave extends to the possession of two wives only, in order that the dignity of freedom may be duly supported."[1] But he may marry four slaves.[2]

If a free man marries five wives by separate contracts, the contract as to the first four is valid, and as to the fifth invalid. If he marries all five by one contract, then all marriages are vitiated. The same rule applies to the case of a slave marrying three wives.

If an infidel, married to five wives, embraces Muhammedanism, there is a difference of opinion as to what effect this will have on his marital rights. If he married them all at once, separation will be effected between him and each of the wives, according to Hanifa and Abu Yusuf—a decision, which implies that if he married them successively the latest marriage becomes invalid. On the other hand

[1] Hidaya Bk. II, ch. I.
[2] Query, Droit Musulman, vol. I, p. 673.

Muhammed and Zufer maintain that the husband will be at liberty to select out of the five any four he may like, in whatever order he may have married them.

g.) *Servile status.*

It is not lawful, and strictly speaking, it is useless for a man to marry his own slave, because legality of enjoyment is as fully secured by the right of property as it could be by a contract of marriage. It is lawful for the master to cohabit with his slave and the children are legitimate if he acknowledges their paternity. But the slave concubine is not on equal basis with the ordinary wife, in that she does not have the same rights as the free wife in regard to separate maintenance and lodging, nor does she receive a dower nor inherit anything of her master's estate except by special bequest. She is, however, emancipated, *ipso facto,* on the death of her master. The author of the Hidaya says that such a union is no valid marriage, because "marriage was instituted with a view that the fruit might belong equally to the father and the mother, and mastership and servitude are contradictory to each other, wherefore it is not admissible that offspring should be divided between the master and the slave."

As to the marriage of a man with a slave woman belonging to another there is a difference of opinion. Shafi'i holds that such a union is unlawful except on two conditions: (1) when the man has not a free wife; (2) when he is unable to pay the dower of a free woman and is afraid of being tempted to commit fornication. Hanifa, on the other hand, maintains that a marriage between a man and a slave other than his own is valid unless he is already married to a free woman, the reason for the exception being it would be humiliating to a free woman to share her husband with a slave partner. Malik maintains that even when a man has a free wife he may marry a slave woman with the free woman's consent. And if he is already married to a slave it is lawful to add another wife who is free.

If a man marries the female slave of another person, and afterwards becomes her owner, in whole or in part, the marriage becomes void. A slave may, however, lawfully be married to the son of her master, but if the master dies the marriage is invalidated because she becomes the property of the son.

Marriage between persons who are permanently prohibited from intermarrying is void *ab initio* or *batil* and creates no civil rights or obligations between the parties. The marriage is considered non-existing in fact as well as in law, and unless the parties dissolve the marriage themselves voluntarily, the court will dissolve it on its own motion.

On the other hand, marriage between persons whose disability to intermarry is temporary is voidable, *fasid.* While such marriages may be annuled by the court when the facts are brought to its notice, they are nevertheless capable of producing certain legal effects; for example, legitimacy of children, right to demand payment of proper dower, *etc.*

III. Equality of Position

1. *General Doctrine of Equality*
Kafa'ah

Kafa'ah literally means equality. In the technical sense it means equality of a man with a woman in six respects.

(1) In point of tribe or family.

(2) In point of religion.

(3) In point of character.

(4) In point of occupation.

(5) In point of fortune.

(6) In point of freedom.

In order that a marriage may bear the character of a suitable union in law, the husband must be the equal of his wife; that is, he must not be inferior to her. The Prophet is said to have declared: "Take ye care that none contract women in marriage but their proper guardians, and that they be so contracted only with their equals." And again: "Cohabitation, society and friendship cannot be completely enjoyed excepting by persons who are each others equals."[1] There is a difference of opinion as to whether equality is requisite on the part of the husband only or is to be demanded as regards both spouses. Hanifa and Abu Yusuf hold the latter opinion; but *Imam* Muhammed maintains, and his is regarded as the better view, that equality is required only on the part of the husband.[1] "As a woman of high rank and family would abhor society and cohabitation with a mean man, it is requisite that regard be had to equality with respect to the husband; that is to say, that the husband be the equal of his wife; but it is not necessary that the wife be the equal of the husband, since men are not degraded by cohabitation with women who are their inferiors."[2] Hence, "if a woman should marry a man better than herself, her guardian has no power to separate them; for he is not disgraced by a man having subject to him one who is not his equal."[3]

The effect of inequality upon marriage is disputed. Hanifa and his disciples hold that it renders the marriage voidable, subjecting it to an attack by the woman's guardians any time before the pregnancy of the woman, "so as to remove the dishonor they might otherwise sustain by it"; but that it is perfectly valid in so far as the parties

[1] Hidaya.
[1] Ibni Abidin, 436.
[2] Hidaya.
[3] Baillie.

themselves are concerned, and that in case of the death of either party the survivor has rights of inheritance. But if there is a misrepresentation, the wife herself may attack. For example, if a man marries a woman, saying that "he is so and so," but it turns out that he is the brother of that so and so, or his paternal uncle, "then the woman shall be entitled to set aside the marriage, although the husband might be her equal."[1] Hassan maintains, on the contrary, that equality is an essential condition of marriage and that a contract between unequals is void.[2] In this view, however, he is in the minority. In order that the guardians of a woman may attack a marriage on the ground of inequality, they must have been ignorant of the marriage at the time it was contracted. If guardians gave their consent or signified in any manner their assent to a marriage, they lose their right of attacking the validity of the contract, even though they were at the time ignorant of the inequality.[1] If a guardian provides a woman with a dower, he will be held to have assented to the marriage and will be barred from raising the question of inequality. Although some jurists have differed from this view, claiming that such conduct does not amount to an acquiescence, the weight of authority is against them. The jurists differ as to what class of guardians are entitled to oppose an unequal marriage. Some hold that only those guardians who are within the prohibitive degrees are entitled to raise the question, but according to others any relative on the paternal side may interpose. It is settled, however, that this power is confined to the agnates and does not belong to the maternal relative.

[1] Kazi Khan.
[2] Ibn Abidin, 436. Mahmud Essad, p. 44. Suleiman Sirri, Hulasat-al-Muhtarin, p. 47.
[3] Compare Al Mudawwana, p. 20.

(1) *Equality in respect to tribe or family.*

This point of distinction is peculiar to the Arabs. According to Suleiman Sirri, other Muhammedan nationalities, such as the Persians and the Turks, among whom tribal distinction is not so marked, may disregard this point of inequality.[1] Mahmud Essad maintains that a common man who establishes his equality with a woman in five other respects may marry her, although she is of the highest aristocracy. Al-Nawawi, however, asserts that according to the better view, this point of equality is to be taken into consideration among the other Muhammedan nationalities just as much as among the Arabs.[2]

Among Koreishites all are equal in point of family; so even if one is not of the family of Hashim, the grandfather of the Prophet, which is considered the noblest family in Arabia, he is equal to a Hashimite. But an Arab who is not a Koreishite is not the equal of a Koreishite. Among Arabs all tribes are in principle equal, except that one who belongs to the tribe of Bahalu, "a tribe notorious for their vices,"[3] is not on an equality with the general body of the Arabs. Some are of opinion that one distinguished by merit is the equal of one of high lineage, so that a lawyer is the equal of a woman descended from Ali, the son-in-law of the Prophet; "but it would be more correct to say that he is not her equal."[4]

(2) *In respect to religion.*

The second point in which equality is of importance is the religion of the man's ancestors. Marriage between a Muhammedan girl and a non-Muhammedan man is, as we have already seen, absolutely prohibited. A man who has embraced Muhammedanism cannot be considered the equal

[1] Hulasat-al-Muhtarin, p. 47.
[2] Minhadj, p. 332.
[3] Kifaya, Vol. II, p. 50.
[4] Fet. Alamkiri.

of a woman whose father is a Muhammedan, and a man whose father is a Muhammedan, but whose mother is not, is not held to be the equal of a woman both of whose parents are Muslims. "A man," however, "who has apostatized from the faith, but has returned to it, is the equal of a person who has never fallen into apostasy."[1]

(3) *In respect to character.*

Inequality in respect of piety and virtue is, according to Hanifa and Abu Yusuf, another ground which gives the guardians a right to attack the marriage; "and this is approved, because virtue is one of the first principles of superiority, and a woman derives a degree of scandal and shame from the profligacy of her husband, beyond what she sustains even from that of her kindred. Muhammed alleges that positive equality in point of virtue is not to be required (as that is connected with religion to which rules regarding merely worldly matters do not apply), and that the rule applies to cases where by base or degrading misconduct (such as exposing himself intoxicated in the public street) the man may have incurred derision and contempt."[2] A person who is unjust or impious (*fasik*) is not the equal of a just woman; nor is he the equal of a woman whose father is just,[3] although she herself is known to be impious, because a woman derives her distinction through her father, and may become pious under the influence of her just father.[4] Equality in this particular is required at the commencement of the marriage, but subsequent inequality does not effect its permanence; so that if a man were the equal of his wife in piety and virtue when he married her, but should afterward become depraved, that would be no ground for cancelling the marriage.

[1] Baillie, Vol. I, p. 63.
[2] Hidaya.
[3] Minhadj.
[4] Mahmud Essad, Kitabi Nikah, p. 471.

(4) *In respect to occupation.*

The fourth point of distinction to be taken into consideration with respect to equality is occupation or business. There is a difference of opinion on this point; some, and among them Hanifa, hold that the character of the man's occupation is not to be taken into consideration unless it is of a degrading nature. Others hold that the occupation in which the prospective husband is engaged must be as nearly as possible on a footing of equality with that in which the family of the bride is engaged;[1] thus persons engaged in trades of a lower sort, such as barbers, horse-dealers, weavers, sweepers and tanners, are not the equals of lawyers, bankers and perfumers, "and it is said that this difference arises owing to difference of times. In the time of Abu Hanifa, on whom be peace, people did not deem any profession objectionable, and regard was had to the goodness of the character of the person no matter to whatever profession he belonged; but this view was changed in the times of his disciples."[2] The principle upon which regard is to be had to occupation or trade is that men derive a certain consequence from the respectability of their callings, whereas a degree of contempt is annexed to them on account of the meanness thereof.[3]

(5) *In respect to fortune.*

Equality with respect to property is not in principle required, but it may be insisted that a man must be able to pay the wife a dower and to support her. According to Shafi'ites this point is not to be insisted upon, and accordingly they take into consideration only five points of inequality, instead of six.[4] According to Hanifites, however, dower is a consideration for the enjoyment of the

[1] Mahmud Essad, p. 48.
[2] Kazi Khan.
[3] Hidaya.
[4] Minhadj, p. 332.

woman and its payment is therefore necessary; and upon the provision of support to the wife depends the permanency of the matrimonial connection, so that this also is indispensable.[1] This requirement of ability to support a wife is fulfilled if it appears that the man has sufficient means for the immediate future—for one month, according to some, and for one year, according to others. There is a disagreement as to whether more emphasis should be laid on ability to support a wife or on ability to pay the dower. Some hold the latter view, while Abu Yusuf says that regard is to be had only to the man's ability to support his wife, because, unlike dower, support can not be postponed. Hanifa and Muhammed, on the other hand, consider "the fortune of the man in general, without regard to any particular ability, so that a man who may be in a position both to pay the dower and to provide subsistence, yet may not be the equal of a woman possessed of a large property; since men consider wealth as conferring superiority, and poverty as inducing contempt." Abu Yusuf, on the other hand, maintains that relative wealth is not to be regarded in this respect, since it is not a thing of a stable or permanent nature, "as property may be acquired in the morning and lost before night."[2]

The view which Abu Yusuf maintains seems to be supported by the better authorities. So Zahir-al-riwayah says that, if a man should not have enough for both support and dower, he is not the equal of his wife, whether she is rich or poor. "No regard is to be had to anything beyond this; so that if he should have enough for these two objects, he is to be considered her equal in respect to property, though she were a person of great wealth." The duty to support his wife devolves on a man only if she is a grown woman, or, if a girl, when she is fit for matri-

[1] Hidaya.
[2] Hidaya.

monial intercourse; "for if she be young and unfit for that purpose, she has no right to maintenance."[1]

(6) *In respect to freedom.*

Equality in freedom is of importance, "because bondage is an effect of infidelity and therein are found the properties of meanness and turpitude."[2] A slave, therefore, cannot be considered the equal of a free woman, nor is one who has been emancipated equal to a woman who has never been a slave.[3] The taint of servile status attaches also to the freedman's son, although he himself be born free; so that a man whose father was emancipated is not the equal of a woman two of whose paternal ancestors were free.

Mahmud Essad says that, just as the requirement of equality in point of tribe or family is peculiar to the Arabs, so the requirement of equality in point of freedom is peculiar to Muhammedans of other nationalities, all Arabs being born free.[4]

"Equality in respect of freedom and Islam is to be regarded in the case of Ajamees (Muhammedans other than Arabs), for they pride themselves in these distinctions and not in lineage. But in the case of Arabs, the Islam of a father is not a condition of equality; * * * but freedom is indispensable to an Arab, for it is not lawful to reduce Arabs to slavery."[5]

Aside from these six qualifications, no other points, such as equality in age, beauty, or understanding, may be taken into account, although certain writers have entertained doubts as to whether some of these matters should not be considered.

Separation for lack of *kafa'at* or equality has to be made

[1] Baillie.
[2] Hidaya.
[3] Minhadj.
[4] Kitabi Nikah, p. 47.
[5] Baillie, p. 64.

before a judge, and until cancelled by the judge the marriage is lawful and binding. Separation, however, is not a repudiation, and therefore, if it takes place before the consummation of the marriage, the husband is not bound to pay any dower (*mahr*); but, if it takes place after consummation, the husband is not only liable to pay the entire dower, but also to furnish whatever sum as is necessary to support the woman during her period of probation (*iddah*).

IV. The Marriage Contract

(1.) *Proposals of Marriage.*

A marriage proposal may be made by any person if neither of the parties is legally incapacitated from entering into a contract of marriage. It is forbidden to demand in marriage a woman who is married to another, or who is undergoing her *iddah*,[1] whether after a separation or after death; but this rule does not apply to a man proposing to his divorced wife if the *iddah* is due to this separation.

It is likewise forbidden to make a proposal to a woman already engaged to another man, even when no dower had as yet been paid, provided the man to whom she is engaged is of good moral character. Whether a person is of good moral character or not is to be judged in accordance with the standard of his own religion. Thus a Muhammedan may not propose to a Christian of Jewish woman already engaged to a man of her own faith, if the latter is of good character. If a marriage is contracted in disregard of this prohibition, then, according to *Malik* such a marriage, if not consummated, is to be annulled, even if the first suitor does not press his claim.

It is lawful, however, to court a woman undergoing *iddah*, and to make covert proposal, saying: "I desire you",

[1] Cf. infra. p. 28.

"Such a one desires you" *etc.*, and even to send her presents, provided they are not sent for her maintenance. To provide maintenance implies wedlock.

According to the Muhammedan law it is not only permitted but also recommended that the suitor see the face and hands of the woman, with her knowledge and consent. This is said to have been recommended by the Prophet himself, who one day meeting a man named Mugire bin Shoda, and learning that he intended to marry a certain woman, told him to go and "look at her, for it will be conducive to the durability of friendship and harmony between you." "The time for seeing her should precede the betrothal. If he is not pleased with her, he should keep silence, and should not say: "I don't want her", or, "She is so and so", lest she feel hurt. The woman is recommended to have a look at the man, if she wants to marry him; because anything that would please her with him will please him with her [*i. e.* both will be pleased with good features] and each of them can renew his or her glances whenever he or she wants, in order to discern the features of his or her object, so that he or she may not repent after marriage."[1]

The promise of future marriage and the mere reading of the *fathihah*,[2] without making a legal contract, does not constitute marriage; and either of the parties may withdraw his or her promise. The woman may retract her consent even after she has accepted presents made by the suitor.

(2) *Consent.*

Marriage is legally established by an offer made by one of the parties and accepted by the other. It does not depend for its validity upon the observance of any religious rite or ceremony.

[1] Abdul Kadir, Al-nahr; p. 218.

[2] The first chapter of the Koran, with the recital of which Muhammedans commonly begin a new undertaking.

According to the Hanifite school of jurists, no fixed words need be used in contracting marriage. Offer and acceptance may be made by literal or plain (*sarih*) words, or by metaphorical and ambiguous (*kinayah*) words. A contract of marriage may be made in the form of a sale; the woman saying: "I have sold myself to thee for so much as dower," and the man saying: "I accept." Similarly in the opinion of this school, a valid marriage is made, if a word importing gift be used. The Shafi'ites, on the other hand, hold that since marriage is a contract which has been legalized for special reasons—preservation of the species, determination of descent, restraint of masculine debauchery, encouragement of chastity, love and union between the husband and the wife and mutual help in earning a livelihood—the words *tazwij* or *nikah,* which definitely and exclusively imply matrimony, can alone constitute such a relation.[1] The Malikites, however, take a position between the two extremes, holding that if the words *tazwij* or *nikah* be used, there is no doubt as to the validity of the marriage, while if other words, such as gift (*hibah*), consignment (*tamlik*), be employed, evidence is admissible to show that the real intention was marriage.

Not only is there difference of opinion between the various schools and among the members of the respective schools, but there is also inconsistency in the different pages of the same work. This comes from the fact that the jurists discuss at great length the words that may be used to enter into a marriage contract and the different formulae of offer and acceptance, but do not lay down any general principles to be applied to particular cases. They all undertake the arduous task of classifying each word in all its grammatical forms and indicating its significance in all possible combinations of formulae. In their interpretation of these formulae, because of their literal adherence to words

[1] Minhadj, p. 318.

and a certain tendency toward subtleties, they have reached results that are admittedly contrary to the policy of the law and in some instances manifestly absurd. For a single example: "The following is reported from Abu Yusuf: A man says to a woman: 'Give thyself in marriage to me for a thousand [coins]'; the woman says: 'I will not do so except for two thousand.' The man then says: 'Fear God and fear Him'; the woman says: 'Verily have I done so.'" The marriage is contracted and becomes binding *ipso facto;* it is not open to the woman to explain whether her expression referred to an acceptance of marriage or to fear of God.[1] From all this mass of casuistry one principle may be inferred: all the schools seem to agree that if the words used do not carry a right of immediate possession, they do not establish a valid marriage.

Marriage contracted in jest (*hazl*) or under duress (*akrah*) is valid and binding. The authority for this is a precept of the Prophet: "There are three things in which it makes no difference whether a man is in earnest or in jest, marriage, divorce and vows."

It is essential to the validity of the marriage contract that the offer and acceptance be expressed at the same meeting or, rather, at the same sitting (*majlis*). Marriage cannot be contracted while walking or riding, but if contracted on board a ship it is valid.[2] It is immaterial how long the sitting may last, provided the attention of the parties is not distracted by any other business or occupation. Any such interruption is regarded as a change of meeting; if, for instance, both parties being present, one of them makes a declaration, and the other then rises or takes to some other occupation before acceptance, there is no contract. And again: "A man says in the presence of two witnesses: 'I have married so and so'; then the intelligence reaches

[1] Kazi Khan.
[2] Mahmud Essad, p. 29.

the woman, it may be in the presence of the same two witnesses, and she accepts the marriage. This is not valid, according to the saying of Abu Hanifa and Muhammed, on whom be peace!"[1] because proposal and acceptance are not made in the same meeting. "But if the man sends to the woman an ambassador, or if he writes to her a letter, saying: 'Verily I have married thee for so much,' and if she accepts the marriage in the presence of two witnesses . . . this is valid";[2] because the ambassador's speech or the reading of the letter amounts to a proposal and the woman accepts it in the same meeting.

No contract of marriage is complete unless the contracting parties understand its nature and reciprocally consent to it. Puberty (*bulugh*) and discretion (*akl*) are, accordingly, essential conditions of capacity to enter a valid marriage contract.

Freedom also is essential to capacity for marriage. A slave cannot enter into a contract of marriage without the consent of his master.[3]

(3) *Consent of guardians.*

The contracting parties must, however, be distinguished from the bride and bridegroom. While an infant (*i. e.*, a child under seven) is disqualified from entering into a marriage contract, the guardian may validly contract marriage for his ward, subject to the ward's approval and ratification when he or she reaches puberty.

When the parties to a marriage contract act for themselves, they must be of legal age and of sound mind. A contract entered into by two minors may, however, be validated by the consent of their respective guardians. If two minors enter into such a contract and live as man

[1] Kazi Khan.
[2] Ibid.
[3] Fet. Alamkiri, Vol. I, p. 377.

and wife without the knowledge of their guardians until one or the other attains puberty, the contract is binding with respect to one or both, as the case may be. "The puberty of a boy is established by the symptoms of puberty. If no such symptoms exist, then when he completes his eighteenth year, according to Abu Hanifa. The puberty of a girl is attained on her having menstrual courses . . . or becoming pregnant . . ; otherwise she attains puberty when she completes her seventeenth year. It is, however, given us as an authoritative decision, according to the opinion of Abu Yusuf, that fifteen years is the age of puberty in the male and female. The reason for this is the shortness of human life in our times."[1]

There is a disagreement between the Hanifites and the Shafi'ites, and also among the Hanifites themselves, as to whether an adult woman, although of sound mind, can contract marriage without the ratification and approval of her guardian. Hanifa and Abu Yusuf hold that she may be married by virtue of her own consent, although the contract may not have been approved by her guardian. Muhammed, of the same school, contends that the contract is not valid, or its validity is suspended, if the guardian of the woman expresses his dissent. Malik and Shafi'i, on the other hand, go still further and hold that a woman may under no circumstances contract herself in marriage, "because the end proposed in marriage is the acquisition of those benefits which it produces, such as procreation and so forth, and if the conclusion of this contract were in any respect committed to women, its end might be defeated, they being of weak reason and open to flattery and deceit."[2]

(4) *Witnesses.*

Marriage is not valid unless it is contracted in the pres-

[1] Al-Nahr.

[2] Hidaya, Fath-al-Karib. p. 431.

ence of two sane, free and male witnesses. According to Hanifites and Shafi'ites, however, one male witness and two female witnesses are sufficient. This alternative is based on the passage in the Koran: " . . . and call to witness two witnesses of your own people; but if there be not two men, let there be a man and two women of those whom ye shall judge fit for witnesses."[1] Malikites, on the other hand, hold that this rule applies to witnesses in ordinary transactions, and is not to be extended to contracts of marriage, in the negotiation of which the presence of two male witnesses is absolutely essential.[2]

Witnesses, according to Hanifa, are required by the Koranic law. They are not called in merely for the purpose of testifying to the conclusion of the contract or to its provisions; their presence is essential to the validity of the transaction. If a man marries a woman, citing as witnesses God and his Prophet, the marriage is void;[3] for "every marriage that takes place is witnessed by God, and some of the learned have held that such a marriage involves blasphemy and infidelity, because it implies a belief that the Prophet knows hidden things, which is blasphemy."[4] This requirement of ceremonial witnesses is peculiar to marriage; in the case of other contracts the presence of witnesses is required only with a view to their giving evidence before the judge.[5] The author of Hidaya says that the presence of witnesses is essential to the validity of marriage, by reason of the saying of the Prophet that "there is no marriage without witnesses." Malik, on the other hand, maintains that witnesses are required in order to secure the publicity of marriage, and that it is publicity which is essential to validity; so that if a man

[1] Sura II, v. 282.
[2] Khalil.
[3] Mahmud Essad. p. 36.
[4] Kazi Khan and Mahmud Essad.
[5] Inaya, Vol. II, p. 1.

marries a woman in the presence of witnesses and stipulates for concealment, the marriage is not valid; but if he marries without witnesses and with the stipulation that there shall be publicity, the marriage is valid. One male or two female witnesses are sufficient for the validity of marriage when a father gives his daughter in marriage, she herself being present. The father, in this case, constitutes the other witness. Similarly, when the father delegates to a third person his power to give his daughter in marriage, the delegate is regarded as a witness.

It is essential that the witnesses to a marriage should be persons capable of contracting marriage for themselves. They must be free, of sound mind, and of mature age. It is likewise "necessary that they should be Mussulmans; the evidence of non-Mussulmans not being legal with respect to Mussulmans." If, however, a Mussulman marries a female *kitabi* (Christian or Jew), Abu Yusuf and Hanifa hold that marriage is rendered lawful by the presence of two *kitabi* witnesses. Muhammed and Zufer, on the other hand, maintain that such witnesses are not lawful, because their testimony with respect to declaration and consent in marriage amounts to evidence, and the evidence of infidels regarding Mussulmans is illegal; "wherefore it is in fact the same as if they had not heard the declaration and consent of the parties. The argument of the two elders, in reply to this objection, is that evidence is required in matrimony, not with any view to the ascertainment of a point of property (such as dower), but merely in order to establish the husband's right of cohabitation, which is in this case the object."[1] All the writers seem to agree that no valid marriage is contracted if the witnesses are pagans, that is, neither Muhammedans, Christians nor Jews.[2]

There is a difference of opinion as to whether witnesses

[1] Hidaya.
[2] Mahmud Essad, p. 37.

to a marriage have to be men of good character. Hanifites are of opinion that the good character of a witness is not an essential condition, and that the presence of impious persons (*fasik*) satisfies the requirements of the law.[1] Shafi'i maintains, however, that marriage may not be contracted in the presence of such witnesses, "because evidence is entitled to reverence and respect, the Prophet having said: 'Pay reverence to witnesses,' and *fasiks* are not proper objects of such reverence, but rather the reverse." "To this our doctors (Hanifites) reply that *fasiks* are competent to act for themselves, and that competency to act as witnesses must appertain to them, since they are not incapacitated from acting with respect to others. A *fasik,* moreover, is capable of holding the office of a Sultan or an Imam, whence it follows that he is also capable of being a witness."[2]

As has been already indicated, marriage witnesses are not ceremonial witnesses only; they must be able to give evidence. Not only, therefore, must they be present at the time of the conclusion of the contract, but they must know its terms. They must be able to testify to the identity of the persons from whom the proposal and consent respectively emanated. If a woman were so concealed or veiled that neither of the witnesses could recognize her, and were not able to tell whether she or any other female in the room gave the consent, their testimony would be insufficient. Therefore, if they are deaf, or sleeping at the time the contract is made, it is not valid. According to Hanifites, a blind person may be a witness; all the other schools, however, hold that sight is as essential a condition as hearing.[3]

[1] Ibn Abidin, pp. 373-376.
[2] Hidaya.
[3] Clavel, Droit Musulman, Vol. VIII, p. 46.

(5) *Marriage Under Condition or Term.*

Marriage is not valid when contracted subject to a condition; that is, subject to any circumstance or event the realization of which is uncertain. For example, if a man were to say: "I marry thee if my father will consent," and the bride were to say: "I consent," there would be no contract. So also with a marriage to take effect at a future time. In both those cases, however, subsequent cohabitation establishes a valid marriage.

When marriage is contracted under an illegal condition, the marriage is valid and the condition void; for instance, a marriage in which the husband stipulates that there shall be no dower.[1] The condition is illegal, and the contract is valid. And again, when a master gives his female slave in marriage to his male slave, and "the male slave begins and says: 'Give this thy female slave in marriage to me for one thousand on condition that the authority in the matter of divorce shall remain with thee, so that thou (the master) shalt divorce her whenever it pleases thee,' and the master gives her in marriage to him, then the marriage shall be valid, but the authority in the matter of divorce shall not vest in the master."[2]

If, however, a man marries a woman for a dower of two thousand *dirhams* if she be handsome and for one thousand if she be ugly, "the learned have said that, according to the opinion of all, the marriage and both the conditions also are valid; so that if she is handsome the dower shall be two thousand *dirhams,* and if she be ugly the dower shall be one thousand."[3]

A usufructuary marriage, that is, a marriage of which the duration is limited to a specific term, cannot be validly contracted. Such marriages are known as *mut'ah* marriages,

[1] See *infra.*
[2] Kazi Khan.
[3] *Ibid.*

and were "admitted by the pre-Islamic institutions, and allowed equally among the Jews and the Arabs at the time the Islamic laws were promulgated, and instances of such unions were not rare even in Christendom. Three days after the Prophet's entry into Mecca these marriages were forbidden by him as contrary to the Islamic principles."[1] The Prophet said: "I had permitted you to enjoy women, but God has prohibited this until the day of reckoning." The institution seems to have been so deeply rooted that, in spite of this express prohibition, Ibn Abbas tried to introduce it after Muhammed's death. But we are told by the author of the Kifayah that "Ali informed him that the Prophet had declared it unlawful, upon which he retracted from his opinion of usufruct being allowable; and Ibn Abbas having thus retracted, all the companions appear to have agreed concerning its illegality."

(6) *Marriage by Guardians.*

The marriage of infants under age or of insane persons by their guardians (*wali*) is lawful, the Prophet having declared that "marriage is committed to the parental kindred." Malikites interpret this to mean that the father only may contract marriage for the child, while the Shafi'ites extend this power to the grandfather. The Hanifites however, argue that any guardians may validly contract marriage for their wards, "lest an opportunity of marrying them be lost." Shafi'i contends that to entrust this power to any other persons than the father and the grandfather would be oppressive, since it is to be supposed that no others are equally interested in the child's welfare and happiness; and it is on this principle that kindred of a more distant degree are not empowered to act with respect to the property of infants." Inasmuch as power over prop-

[1] Seyid Amir Ali, p. 309. Perron: Femmes Arabes, p. 171. Compare: Code Rabbinique, Vol. II, p. 232.

erty is a matter of far less importance than that over persons, it follows *a fortiori* that when the former power is excluded the latter must also be denied. On the other hand: "Our doctors (Hanifites) argue that kinship is a cause of affection in other relatives just as in parents, and, in whatever degree affection may be lacking, a provision is made against any evil consequence by vesting in the child after puberty an option of acquiescence in the match, which acquiescence is necessary to establish its validity—[a rule] contrary to that which governs acts [of guardians] with respect to property."[1]

The Shafi'ites further contend that no guardian of a widow (*sayibeh*), not even a father or grandfather, may validly contract marriage for his ward. They argue that her experience of matrimony is to be considered as endowing her, although still a minor, with sufficient capacity and understanding to act and judge for herself. "To this our doctors (Hanifites) reply," says the author of Hidaya, "that the ward requires a guardian, whose tenderness and affection must be necessarily admitted; neither can her acquaintance with the other sex be considered as endowing her with any additional portion of understanding in regard to mankind, without concupiscence, which in a minor does not exist. It may also further be observed that the precept of the Prophet already quoted is general and indiscriminate, and therefore includes all relatives equally; which makes it a sufficient answer to Malik and Shafi'i."

(7) *Marriage by Proxy.*

Under the Muhammedan law it is permissible to the spouses to contract marriage by proxy. The agent may be of either sex, and must be capable of contracting a marriage for himself or herself; *i. e.,* the agent must have reached

[1] Hidaya.

the age of puberty and must be sane.[1] In the appointment of an agent for the purpose of marriage no witnesses are necessary.

Agency to contract marriage may be general or special. It is general when the authority given is a power to select a husband or a wife; it is special if the authority is to contract marriage with a particular person. If the authority is general, there is a difference of opinion as to whether the agent of a woman may contract her to himself, or to any of his own relatives, unless expressly empowered to that effect. Some authorities hold that the contract is valid,[2] others hold that it is not.[3] If the authority is in any way limited, there can be no deviation from its terms. "If a person appoints another his agent (*wakil*), for the purpose of giving him in marriage to a woman, and if the *wakil* then gives him in marriage to his own daughter, and if the daughter is a minor, the marriage is not valid according to all the three Imams, that is, Abu Hanifa, Abu Yusuf and Muhammed, because the authority referred to a woman, and here the *wakil* married the person [his principal] to a minor. If she has attained puberty, then, according to Abu Hanifa, on whom be peace, the same result follows, because the *wakil* has apparently acted in his own interest rather than that of the principal; but according to the two disciples, Yusuf and Muhammed, the marriage is valid. If the *wakil* gives the principal in marriage to his [the *wakil's*] sister, who has attained puberty,[4] then, according to all, the marriage is valid, because the sister is not so closely related as the daughter and comes within the authority conferred."[5]

If the agent of a woman gives his principal in marriage

[1] Mahmud Essad, p. 68.
[2] See Kazi Khan.
[3] Baillie, p. 76.
[4] See Fetawa Alemkiri, Vol. II, pp. 415 and 416.
[5] Kazi Khan.

to one who is not her equal the marriage is not valid, but if the man is the equal of the woman it is valid, even if the person to whom the woman has been married is blind or a cripple. But if the agent acted *mala fide* toward the principal, by marrying her to an eunuch, the marriage is invalid.

An unauthorized person may enter into a contract of marriage for another, and such a marriage will become valid if ratified by the parties concerned. This at least is the view of the Hanifites. Shafi'i, however, disagrees and maintains that all acts of an unauthorized agent are null, "because the use of a contract is for the purpose of establishing its effect, like that for sale, for instance, which is used for the purpose of establishing a right of enjoyment; and an unauthorized agent (*fuzuli*) is incapable of establishing the effect, on account of his want of authority; wherefore the act of a *fuzuli* is nugatory. [On the other hand] the argument of our doctors (Hanifites) is, that the foundation of the contract, namely, the declaration and acceptance, has been laid by a competent person, and has reference to its proper subject; neither can any injury be sustained if the contract be executed, inasmuch as there exists in respect to it a person who has a right of assent, and who, if he think proper, will signify such assent, and give the contract force, or, if otherwise, will reject it. And in reply to what is urged by Shafi'i we observe that the effect of a contract is sometimes deferred to a period subsequent to the time or date of the contract.[1]

The authorities are agreed that one person, if properly authorized, can act in a marriage as agent for both parties, and that the contract becomes binding when he openly declares: "I have married my principal X to my principal Y." There is a difference of opinion, however, as to whether one person can act on both sides as an unauthorized agent (*fuzuli*). Hanifa and Muhammed are of opinion that such

[1] Hidaya.

a marriage will be validated by ratification; but Abu Yusuf maintains that one person cannot act as *fuzuli* on behalf of both parties. He maintains also that a person may not act at once as *fuzuli* and as principal; *i. e.*, if a person marries himself to another without the other's authorization, the contract cannot be validated by ratification.

Agency is terminated by the death of either the agent or the principal. It is also terminated by the marriage of the principal, even though no notice of such marriage is given to the agent.

V. Dower (Mahr)

Mahr is an ante-nuptial settlement upon a woman of a sum of money or other property, to which she becomes entitled by marriage. This dower in Muhammedan law differs essentially from the *dos* of the Roman or the dower of English law. It is said to have derived its origin from the Jewish law, according to which the specification of a dotal debt is essential to a marriage contract. At Muhammedan law, however, while the constitution of a dower is essential to marriage, specification of dower is not essential. If no dower be specified, and even if it be expressly stipulated that there shall be no dower, the wife is entitled to a reasonable dower. Another difference is that among the Muhammedans a portion of the dower usually vests at once in the wife, while among the Jews the dower was never made over to the wife for her exclusive use before the dissolution of the marriage.

Dower in Muhammedan law resembles the *donatio propter nuptias* of Roman law. Among the Romans, however, the *donatio* was absolutely voluntary, while in Muhammedan law dower is invariably established, either by contract or by the law. Among the Romans, moreover, the *donatio* usually remained in the hands of the husband during marriage.

The English dower grew out of the purchase marriage, and was originally the price paid for the wife. Whatever may have been its origin among the Arabs, Muhammedan jurisprudence refuses to recognize dower as price or even as consideration. Dower is a result of marriage imposed by law, "merely as a token of respect for its object, the woman."[1]

Anything that is property (*mal*) and has value may be given to or settled upon the wife as dower. There must, of course, be realizable value; dower cannot consist of fish in the sea, birds in the air, or runaway slaves; but it is not essential that the property be tangible; choses in action or any other intangible property may be assigned as dower. There is a difference of opinion as to whether services may be regarded as lawful dower. If a free man marries a woman and the dower is stipulated to be that the man is to serve her for a particular period, or to "teach her the Koran," Abu Yusuf and Hanifa hold that such a stipulation is invalid and that the husband is bound to provide a reasonable dower. Muhammed, however, holds that in such a case the woman is to receive a sum amounting to the estimated value of his services for one year. But if the husband be a slave, such dower is lawful, and the woman is entitled to the stipulated services only. Shafi'i, on the other hand, maintains that in either case the woman is entitled only to the stipulated services, "because whatever may be lawfully received as a fixed return is capable of constituting a dower, since a mutual exchange may be thereby effected, and consequently the case is the same as if the man had married the woman on condition of a stated service to be performed by another person, or on a stipulation that he himself should watch her flocks for a stated

[1] Hidaya.

period." In answer to this the Hanifites argue that "the possession of a woman's person is not to be sought except in return of property; and the teaching of the Koran (or watching the flocks) is not adequate property; neither does right to service, in the opinion of our doctors, constitute property, because it is not substantial or permanent. . . . Service, therefore, not being property, to seek the possession of a woman's person in return for services of a free man is unlawful."[1] But the service of a slave is considered property, even by the Hanifites, "because this comprehends a surrender or delivery of the slave's person, and the person of a slave is actual property . . . wherefore it is analogous to the bestowing of the slave himself as a dower; but with a husband who is free this cannot be the case."[2]

It would seem that this doctrine is in conflict with the following passage from the Koran: "And Thuaih said unto Moses: 'Verily I will give thee one of my two daughters in marriage, on consideration that thou serve me for hire eight years; and if thou fulfill ten years, it is in thine own breast, for I seek not to impose a hardship on thee; and thou shalt find me, if God please, a man of probity.' Moses answered: 'Let this be the covenant between me and thee; whichsoever of the two terms I shall fulfill, let it be no crime in me if I then quit thy service; and God be witness of that which we say.'" But this stipulation for a number of years of service, it will be observed, was not a dower, but a consideration for the covenant with the father, which is entirely independent of the obligation to provide the woman with dower. "And if a man marries a woman on condition that he shall give to the father of the woman a thousand *dirhams,* she shall be entitled to her dower whether he gives to her father a thousand or not."[3]

[1] Hidaya.
[2] Hidaya.
[3] Kazi Khan.

In addition to a sum of money or some other tangible property, a dower may include the doing of a thing. Thus, for example, a man may undertake to pay a certain sum of money and also to repudiate a certain woman to whom he is married. This is not a mere promise, but a part of the act of marriage. If it were a promise to repudiate the prior marriage, the repudiation would not take effect until actually pronounced; but in this case as soon as the contract is made the prior wife is *ipso facto* repudiated. If in case of reciprocal marriages, where a man gives his daughter in marriage to another on condition that the other party shall give him his daughter or sister, it is stipulated that this arrangement shall take the place of dower as regards each wife, it is held by Shafi'i that both contracts are unlawful, because they make one-half of each woman's person a dower and the other half the subject of the marriage. Such bargain is, according to Shafi'i, a nullity. The Hanifites, however, maintain that both the marriage contracts are valid, but that each wife is entitled to a proper dower.

Dower, as already noted, may also consist of choses in action; for example, money owed to the husband by a third which so and so owes him, the marriage is valid, and she has the option, if it pleases her, to make the husband liable person. "If a man marries a woman for a thousand *dirhams* for the thousand, or, if it pleases her, she may proceed against the debtor, insisting that the husband appoint her as his attorney (*wakil*) to collect or release the debt. And if he marries her on condition of his releasing so and so, who owes him a debt, then the debtor is released, and she shall be entitled to her proper dower from the husband, because the release of a third person does not amount to property; so that the case will be treated as if dower were not specified, and, therefore, she will get her proper dower. If, however, she herself was released from a debt, that would be dower, and she will not be entitled to her proper dower in addition."[1]

There are no hard and fixed rules as to the amount of dower. It is usually a matter of agreement between the parties. The early Hanifite jurists fixed the minimum amount at ten *dirhams,* about one and one-half dollars. Malik sets the minimum at a quarter of a *dinar,* or three *dirhams.* Shafi'i, on the other hands, maintains that the amount of the dower, provided it be not purely nominal, like a single grain of wheat, is to be left entirely to the will of the parties, "because the dower is the right of the woman, and consequently it must depend upon herself to determine the amount of it." Any amount above the minimum is lawful, but all the schools strongly recommend moderation, and some have declared that a dower may not legally exceed the dower which the Prophet bestowed on his wives, the *mahral-Sunnah.* The husband may then make the dower "so much of gold as an ox hide can contain."[2]

If an amount lower than the minimum of ten *dirhams* has been agreed upon by the parties, Hanifa, Abu Yusuf and Muhammed hold that the woman is entitled to the minimum amount, while Zufer, another disciple of Hanifa, holds that she is entitled to a proper dower, "because where the sum specified is so small as not to bear the construction of a dower it is the same as if none whatever had been named. "In support of the prevailing Hanifite opinion, however, it is argued that "the impropriety of naming or stipulating so small a sum is on account of the injunction of the law, which cannot be fulfilled with less than ten *dirhams,* and the woman will certainly be satisfied with ten *dirhams,* as she had agreed to accept less than ten."[3] Accordingly, if the husband marries for less than ten *dirhams,* the wife shall be entitled to have the dower completed to

[1] Kazi Khan.
[2] Al-Nahr.
[3] Hidaya.

ten *dirhams;* and no increase shall be made over the ten *dirhams,* although her proper dower might be more than ten *dirhams.*"[1]

If, however, no mention is made of the amount, or if it is expressly agreed that there shall be no dower, the woman is entitled to the proper and customary dower (*mahral-mithl*). What is proper and customary depends upon the birth, rank, wealth and accomplishments of the bride. There is an enormous amount of literature dealing with this question. In determining birth and rank, some writers take into account only the father, his ancestors and collaterals; others include the mother and her relatives; others again, introduce further considerations. From the point of view of a lawyer acquainted with the Western systems of jurisprudence, these discussions are of little importance. It is sufficient to say that the wife is entitled to a "reasonable amount," or to the "dower of her equals." In applying this principle, it is obvious that the more factors one takes into consideration, the nearer he will come to finding out what is the "proper dower"—a subject which gave so much trouble to the early Muhammedan jurists and their commentators.

Whenever there is doubt as to the amount of the dower or there is lack of specification, the wife is entitled to proper dower. Hence, if a man says to a woman: "I marry thee for *dirhams*" without mentioning the number of the *dirhams,* she shall be entitled to her proper dower. Or if a man marries a woman for whatever amount of dower she shall demand, the marriage shall be valid, and it is competent to her to demand payment to the extent of the proper dower . . . and if the marriage takes place with the stipulation that the determination is left to or is in the option of the husband, that is, if the dower is whatever the husband shall decide, then his decision to pay her proper

[1] Kazi Khan.

dower or more is valid; but if his decision is to pay less than her proper dower, it shall not be valid."[1] If a man marries a woman "for less than a thousand" and her proper dower is more than that amount, the dower shall be one thousand. If a man marries a woman and fixes by way of dower two things, one of which is property and the other a promise to do some act, for example, to take her out of town or to divorce a co-wife, and if he fails to fulfill this latter promise, the wife shall be entitled to her proper dower. If the stipulation is that the amount is to be fixed by a stranger, the assignment of dower is defective and proper dower accrues. When the thing mentioned as dower is not in existence, as the future produce of certain trees, or the children of a slave, the assignment is again defective and the woman is entitled to her proper dower.

Dower may be payable immediately, in which case it is called demand dower (*mu'ajjal*); or it may be payable on dissolution of the marriage by the death of the husband or by divorce, in which case it is called deferred dower (*mu'ejjal*); or it may, as is usually the case, be partly on demand (*mu'ajjal*) and partly deferred (*mu'ejjal*). Whether it is one or the other or both depends upon the terms of the contract. In the absence of any agreement, according to Mahmud Essad, the dower is deemed to be deferred.[2] Others, however, maintain that it depends upon the custom of the country. If the dower is on demand, it becomes payable upon the consummation of the marriage or upon a "valid retirement." If the husband divorces the wife before either a consummation or retirement, she receives half of her specified dower; since God has declared: "If ye divorce them before ye have touched them, and have already settled a dower on them, ye shall give them half of what ye have settled . . . but if ye yield up the whole, it will approach

[1] Kazi Khan.
[2] Kitabi Nikah, pp. 86 and 87.

nearer unto piety. And forget not liberality among you, for God seeth what you do." Shafi'i maintains that the dower is not due unless the marriage is consummated, and that a valid retirement entitles the woman merely to a moiety of the dower; but the Hanifite jurists answer that "the woman has completed her part of the contract, by delivering her person and by removing all obstructions, which is the extent of her ability; her right to recompense is, therefore, established and confirmed in the same manner as in a case of sale, where, if the seller has offered the delivery of the goods sold and there is nothing to obstruct possession on the part of the purchaser and the latter neglects to take possession, he is considered as having taken possession, and the thing purchased is afterwards as a trust in the hands of the seller and the payment of the full price is obligatory upon the purchaser."[1]

There is a "valid retirement" when there is no physical obstacle to consummation, and when no third party is present—not even a blind or sleeping person, nor even a dog.[2] according to Abu Hanifa there is a valid retirement if the woman enter a room where her husband is sleeping, whether he is aware of her entrance or not. There is a valid retirement also where the husband is impotent. But if the disability is legal there is no retirement.

In case the dower is on demand the wife may refuse to cohabit with her husband or to go on a journey with him until she receives her dower; but if the dower is deferred, she has no such right. If the husband has connection with the wife and then refuses to pay the dower, there is a difference of opinion as to whether she can be forced to submit to the authority of the husband. Abu Hanifa is of opinion that even after the marriage is consummated, she

[1] Hidaya.

[2] Kazi Khan says if the dog belongs to the husband it does not prevent a "valid retirement."

may refuse to treat him as her husband until the dower has been paid; while his disciples, Abu Yusuf and Muhammed, maintain that she has no right of resistance after she has once yielded herself, "as in a case of sale, where the seller, having delivered the article sold to the purchaser before receiving the price, has no further right over it."[1]

It is permissible to increase the dower after the marriage has been contracted; and, according to Abu Yusuf, if an addition is made to the dower and if then the wife is repudiated before the marriage is consummated, she is entitled to one-half of the additional dower. Zufer, on the other hand, is of opinion that this additional dower is nothing but a gift and, therefore, is of no effect until possession is delivered.

Under the Muhammedan law, as will be explained more fully below, a woman, whether married or single, can hold property in her own right, and if of age is competent to dispose of it. She may, therefore, deal with her father or with her husband.

Accordingly, when a woman has once taken possession of her dower, she may make a present of it to her husband, "because after the execution of the contract, it is her sole right" to dispose of it in any manner she may please; and neither her guardian nor her father has any right to interfere. It follows, *a fortiori,* that an acceptance on her part of any property in lieu of her dower is valid and effective. The wife may lend her dower to her husband, and if he fails to pay it back, she may sue him in her own name or may appoint an attorney to recover the debt.

Another ante-nuptial settlement, which is usually made by the father of the bride, is what in Roman law would be called a *dos,* namely, the *jihaz.* One difference is that while in a Roman marriage it was obligatory on the

[1] Hidaya. Malik agrees with the latter view.

father to provide his daughter with a *dos*, in Muhammedan law there is some doubt as to how far the provision of *jihaz* is obligatory. Whether any such obligation rests upon the father depends upon the custom of the community. It is less clearly a legal obligation in Hanifite countries than among Shafi'ites and Malikites. In practice, however, the giving of a *dos* by the father is quite as usual in the one sect as in the other and is regarded as of equal moral obligation. In those communities where the providing of a suitable *dos* is not obligatory, the father is entitled to spend the dower in the purchase of the *dos*. He "may sell a slave delivered by the husband in order to provide the trousseau. On the question as to whether he may sell real property given as dower there are two opinions."[1] In such cases, of course, the father is not acting for himself, but for his daughter. He will be held to an accounting and will be forced to restore the residue of the dower to his daughter.[2] A trousseau once given to the bride becomes her own property; the father cannot reclaim it unless it appears that it was merely lent. If a man of average means gives clothes or any other wearing apparel to his daughter, and then claims that he had merely lent them for the purpose of the marriage, he will be called upon to swear to the truth of this statement and his oath will be taken as conclusive. If, however, the father is a man of large means, the daughter will be called upon to swear that the property was given to her outright.[3] But no claim made by the bride's father, that other articles delivered to her at the time of marriage with her trousseau were merely lent, will be entertained if preferred after the expiry of a year and if unsupported by witnesses.[4]

[1] Khalil, Mukhtasar.
[2] Clavel, Droit Musulman.
[3] Fetawai Ali Effendi, pp. 57 and 58.
[4] Khalil, Mukhtasar.

PART II

THE MATRIMONIAL RELATION

Marriage creates mutual rights and obligations between the spouses.

Prior to the Islamic legislation, and especially among the pagan Arabs, women had no *locus standi* in the law. The pre-Islamic Arab customs treated them in a harsh manner. Daughters and wives had no rights of inheritance,[1] wives were considered as chattels and passed to the husband's heirs as a part of his estate.[2] The Koran effected a revolution in the condition of women.[3] Muhammed proclaimed as one of the essential teachings of his creed respect for women; he allowed them rights, secured them privileges, and put them on a footing of equality with men in so far as this was practicable. The Koran declares: "Women ought to behave toward their husbands in like manner as their husbands behave towards them, according to what is just;"[4] and Muhammed in his discourse on the *Jabal Arafat* confirms this precept in eloquent terms: "O men, ye have rights over your wives and your wives have rights over you."[5]

In Muhammedan law infidelity to the marriage bond is made more culpable than it had been by custom. The rule is not one-sided; fidelity to bed is inculcated on both sides; it is required equally from man and woman.[6]

[1] Caussin de Perceval, Hist. des Arabes, Vol. III, p. 337.
[2] Sautayra, Droit Musulman, Vol. I, p. 178.
[3] For an exhaustive consideration of the effect of Muhammedanism on the status of women, see Perron, Femmes Arabes avant l'Islamisme et depuis l'Islamisme, especially pp. 170 and 171.
[4] Sura II, v. 228.
[5] Sautayra, Droit Musulman, Vol. I, p. 178, and Durr-al-Mukhtar, Vol. II, p. 1062.
[6] Sautayra, Vol. I, p. 179.

The rights and duties of husband and wife depend upon the terms of the marriage contract, and may be defined in any manner agreed upon between the parties. But there are some consequences of the marriage relation which can not be excluded by contract and others which are considered to be implied, in default of express stipulation or manifest implication to the contrary.

I. Duties of the Husband

The husband is obliged to treat his wife with kindness, and to live on good terms with her, to maintain her in a manner suitable to his wealth, and to make a just division of time and attention, *i. e.*, if he has more than one wife he is bound to act impartially towards each of them.

The Muhammedan law recommends and holds that it is praiseworthy for a husband to cohabit with his wife, but he is legally bound to do so only once during the subsistence of the marriage.[1]

It is, however, incumbent upon a husband to spend some of his time in company of his wife. So if a man continues to say his prayers all night, and to fast the whole day, or spends his time in the company of his female slaves, the woman has recourse to the judge; the judge shall order that the husband shall live for some nights with her and shall give up some of his fasting for her. "And Abu Hanifa, on whom be peace, at first reserved one day and night for the wife, and allowed three days and nights for the husband for the purposes of his fast and prayers; but afterwards withdrew from this opinion, and said that the husband shall be ordered to have regard for his wife, and please and satisfy her with his company for some days and

[1] Durr-al-Mukhtar, Vol. II, p. 432, and Clavel, Droit Musulman, Vol. I, p. 135. Compare Sautayra: Droit Musulman, Vol. I, pp. 179 and 180.

at some times, without holding that there is any fixed time for this purpose."[1]

Muhammedan law prescribes absolute equality in the treatment of wives in all matters. The Koran expressly provides: "If you fear you cannot act impartially (toward your wives) then marry only one." The obligation for making equal division is obligatory whether the husband is potent or impotent, sick or healthy. The Prophet is said to have declared: "The man who hath two wives, and who in partition inclines particularly to one of them, shall in the day of judgment incline to one side" (that is to say, shall be paralytic).[2]

But what is obligatory on the part of the husband in regard to his wives is only in matters lying within his power, as for example living with them, with the object of giving the wives his company and affection, and not in matters which do not lie within his control, because love is a function of the heart and sexual intercourse springs from desire, and neither of these is under the will of the husband.[3] In confirmation of this it is recorded that Ayesha, one of the wives of the Prophet, said that Muhammed made such equal partition of cohabitation among his wives, saying: "Oh God, I thus make an equal partition as to what is in my power, do not, therefore, bring me to account for that which is not in my power."[4]

The duties of the husband are to be observed in respect to all his wives, without distinction between the one who comes to him a virgin and the one married before, between those long married and those married recently, or between the Muslim wife and that Christian or Jewish wife. Shafi'i, however, maintains that when a man already married marries a new wife, he is entitled to live with her for seven

[1] Kazi Khan.
[2] Hidaya, Bk. II, Ch. 6.
[3] Kazi Khan.
[4] Hidaya.

days if she is a virgin, or, if otherwise, three days, and after this period it is incumbent upon him to observe equality between the new and the old wives.[1]

The share of a husband's society to which a wife is entitled is elaborately computed in the Arabic text, but it hardly seems necessary to go into details. It is left to the husband to determine the necessary partition. He may pass a period of twenty-four hours, three or seven days in whatever order of turn he himself shall fix and establish. But this is a partition of residence only, and implies no obligation, as noted above, in matters not in his power.[2]

A wife may abandon her rights in favor of a co-wife, but she is at liberty to resume them whenever she pleases. To enter into an arrangement for the partition of the husband's society for a mercenary consideration is illegal. If a sum has been paid or a present made for such a purpose, the wife may take back the payment or gift.

If, however, a man has a wife who is sneered at on account of her old age, and the husband intends to change her for a young woman, *i. e.*, intends to divorce the old wife and marry the young woman, and if in such case the old wife proposes that he retain her instead of divorcing her, and also marry another wife, and that he live with the new wife for a number of days, and with her, the first wife, for one day, and if the husband marries a new wife on this understanding, "this arrangement is valid and binding."[3] This is confirmed by the Koran which says: "If the wife fears that the husband may become displeased with her, or may turn away from her, it shall be no crime in them if they arrange the matter amicably between themselves; for a reconciliation is better than a separation."

Whenever the husband goes on a journey there shall be

[1] Al-Nahr, p. 100.
[2] Hidaya.
[3] Kazi Khan.

no question of partitioning his time. The husband can take with him whichever wife he chooses; but it is better to cast lots. On his return none of his wives can require him to pass with them the same number of nights that he passed with the wife whom he took with him on his journey. But Shafi'i holds that if the husband goes on a journey without casting lots, then the period of journey with one wife shall be counted in favor of the other wife, and then the husband shall live with the other wife for a like period.

If the husband is taken ill in a house in which no one of his wives lives, he may ask each in turn to come to him. But if he is taken ill in the house of one of his wives, he may remain there until his recovery; on condition that after recovery he shall pass an equivalent period of time with his other wife.[1]

The husband is bound to maintain his wife, whether she belongs to the Moslem faith or not, rich or poor, old or young, so long as she is able to fulfill the primary object of marriage. But when the wife is too young for matrimonial intercourse, she has no right to maintenance from her husband.[2] If, however, the husband be an infant, and, therefore, incapable of generation, and the wife be an adult, she is entitled to her maintenance at his expense, because in this case delivery of the person has been performed on her part, and the obstacle to intercourse is on the part of the husband.[3]

This obligation of the husband comes into operation after the marriage contract has been entered into and the wife is subjected to marital control. It continues in force during the conjugal union, and in some cases also after the union is dissolved.[4]

Nafakah, or maintenance, literally means what a man

[1] Code of Muhammedan Personal Law, Kadri Pasha, p. 42.
[2] Kazi Khan.
[3] Majma', Vol. I, p. 383.
[4] Sautavra enumerates four cases, see Droit Musulman, p. 182.

spends on his family;[1] in the law it signifies all those things which are necessary to the support of life, such as food, clothes and lodging; but "many confine it solely to food."[2]

The duty of maintenance springs from three causes; marriage, relationship and possession—"the maintenance of one of the children of Adam or of animals held in possession"[3]—in other words, held as property. But what concerns us here is only the first—the duty of a husband to maintain his wife by reason of marriage. It is incumbent upon a husband to support his wife whether the marriage is consummated or not, provided consummation is physically possible. The wife is entitled to maintenance although she refuses to surrender herself until she receives the dower, unless the dower is deferred by agreement, or the husband has stipulated for the consummation before the time of payment arrives. If the dower is so deferred or there is such a stipulation, she has no right to deny herself, and if she does she will be considered "rebellious" and, therefore, not entitled to maintenance. The wife is likewise entitled to maintenance, though she is resident in her father's house, unless without valid reason she refuses to comply with the husband's request to reside in his house. This seems to be the opinion of the commentators of the *Zahir-al-riwayah* and the *Mabsut,* although Shafi'i holds that she is not entitled till actual removal; and the author of the *Hidaya,* although an ardent Hanifite, agrees with the latter, for he says the right of maintenance is the consequence of submission or restraint[4]—thus placing maintenance of a wife on the same footing as that of a person who is imprisoned on account of a debt due to another and is, therefore, entitled to maintenance from his creditor.

If a woman whom a man has married is the slave of

[1] Fetnwai Feizlé, p. 173.
[2] Hidaya.
[3] Al-Nahr, p. 174.
[4] Habs, or imprisonment.

another, she is entitled to maintenance, provided her master assigns a separate residence to her, where the husband and his wife may retire without the master calling for the services of the female slave. If the master has assigned a separate residence to her, which means that he will not ask for her services, and if afterwards it "occurs to him to use her services, he shall be entitled to do so, but the husband of the female slave shall no longer be liable to maintain her."[1]

Where a wife, after the marriage has been consummated, falls sick, she is entitled to maintenance whether she is in her husband's house or her father's, even if the sickness renders her unfit for sexual intercourse. "This is upon a principle of benevolence, as analogy would suggest that she is not entitled to maintenance, where she falls sick so as to be incapable of admitting her husband to the conjugal embrace, since in this case she cannot be deemed in custody for the purpose of enjoyment; but the reason for a more favorable construction of the law in this case is that she still remains in custody, as her husband may associate with her, and she may continue to superintend the domestic concerns."[2] The husband, however, is not bound to bear any expenses other than simple maintenance. The cost of medicines purchased during her sickness should come out of her own property; but if the husband pays on her behalf the price of medicines and the doctor's fees, he is a volunteer and cannot recover anything from her; and if she has no property, he is morally bound to pay as an act of succor to one in distress. In this last case, however, he can recover such outlays from her when she becomes solvent, unless he has intended to act benevolently.[3] But if the wife falls sick before consummation of the marriage, she is not entitled to maintenance.

[1] Kazi Khan.
[2] Hidaya, Bk. IV, Ch. 15.
[3] Al-Nahr.

If the husband has intercourse with the wife in her own house, and she then falls sick of a disease, so that she is not able to sustain intercourse, and if while she is sick she goes to her husband's house, then the husband has the option either to retain her in his house, in which case he shall be bound to maintain her, or to send her back to her home, in which case he shall not be bound to maintain her.[1]

If, after intercourse in her husband's house, a wife falls sick and causes herself to be taken to her father's house, she is entitled to maintenance so long as it is found impossible to remove her; but if her removal is possible and she refuses to return without a valid reason, she loses her right to maintenance.[2]

A wife cannot be compelled to accompany her husband on a journey; and if she refuses to do so she retains her right of support during the husband's absence. The wife in such cases has a right to apply for a decree authorizing her to spend a reasonable amount for her maintenance. If supplies have been left in the house, such as money, or food, or cloth suitable for apparel, the judge may direct her to take from such supplies what is needed for her maintenance. And when the absent husband has left property in the hands of a third party, maintenance may be decreed to her from such property, whether it be held in trust or on deposit for him. If no supplies or funds be found from which maintenance may be drawn, she may pledge her husband's credit or use her own separate property. In the latter case she has a claim against the husband after his return for the money used or expended;[3] but unless she has first obtained a judicial decree to that effect, she is not entitled to any reimbursement either from her husband or his heirs. Con-

[1] Kazi Khan.
[2] Ibid.
[3] Fĕtawai Ali Efendi, p. 117.

sequently no action may be brought for arrears of maintenance. When a woman sues her husband for maintenance for a time antecedent to any order of the judge or mutual agreement of the parties, the judge cannot decree maintenance for the past. So also when she contracts debt for the purpose of maintenance; if she has contracted before obtaining a judicial decree, she alone is responsible, and the creditor cannot have recourse against the husband; while if she has contracted with the judge's permission, she can transfer the responsibility to her husband so as to give her creditor a right of action against him.[1]

The husband when undergoing a term of imprisonment is not released from his obligation to pay for his wife's maintenance, even when this imprisonment is for a debt due to his wife which he is unable to pay.[2] The same is true when he is in the Sultan's jail (as distinguished from the judge's jail, or civil jail) by reason of oppression.[3] If, on the other hand, the wife is imprisoned or abducted, maintenance is not due to her during the term of imprisonment. unless it is the husband who has caused her arrest for the debt due to himself. "But if he finds in the prison a room in which he can reach her (and have intercourse with her), then the learned lawyers have said that she is entitled to maintenance from him."[4]

The wife who travels or undertakes a pilgrimage without being accompanied by her husband, has no right to maintenance, even if she travels with one of her relations within the prohibitive degrees. Abu Yusuf, however, thinks that if the wife is undertaking the indispensable pilgrimage[5] she is justified in leaving him and, therefore, is entitled to

[1] Fet. Alemkiri.
[2] Bahr, Vol. IV, pp. 196 and 197. Majma', Vol. I, p. 386.
[3] Kazi Khan.
[4] Kazi Khan.
[5] It is incumbent upon all Muhammedans to perform at least one pilgrimage to Mecca, and this is reckoned among the Faraiz or sacred ordinances.

maintenance. If the husband travels and takes her with him, she has a claim against him for the traveling and lodging expenses.

When the wife undertakes the journey and takes her husband with her, he must defray her living but not her traveling expenses.

There is a difference of opinion as to the factors to be taken into consideration in fixing the amount and the nature of maintenance. Shafi'i contends that the condition of the husband alone is to be regarded, and fixes the amount at two *muds* for a rich person, one and a half *muds* for a person of ordinary means and one *mud* in the case of a poor husband. On the other hand Hanifites hold that "this view is not correct; because what is necessary on account of maintenance is a sufficiency, and what is a sufficiency differs with the difference of individuals and times."[2]
to be supplied, on account of maintenance, according to Hidaya; "what is obligatory on the husband is a sufficiency of maintenance with propriety and decency, without extravagance and superfluity or niggardliness and stint." In support of this theory the Hidaya cites a case where a woman applied to Muhammed for his judgment on this point, and he replied: "Take from the property of your husband whatever may suffice for the subsistence of yourself and your children in the customary way."[3]

Kazi Khan tells us what "the customary way" is. As the husband is liable to provide a sufficiency of bread, so is he also liable to provide a sufficiency of meat; "because according to ha it bread cannot be eaten unless accompanied with meat." This is the best food which a man can provide for his family; "and the medium of what a man may

[1] A certain measure with which corn is measured equal to a pint and one-third of the standard of Baghdad.
[2] Kazi Khan.
[3] Hidaya.

be able to provide for his family is bread and olive; and the lowest food which a man may provide is bread and milk. But as to oil, it is necessary to provide the same, especially in hot countries. And all this is according to the practice of the Arabs. But according to our practice, the maintenance of the wife differs according to the difference in the circumstances of the people and the difference in times."

The Hanifite jurists further hold that in fixing the amount of maintenance due regard must be paid to the respective conditions of both the husband and wife, and not the husband alone, as contended by Shafi'i. Where both are rich, the husband shall allow maintenance on a generous scale, but "without superfluity in the same." When they are both poor, the allowance shall be simple "without stint in it."

Where the husband is a man of means and "eats *huwara* and fried game, and *bajjah,* but the woman is poor and was accustomed to eat barley bread in her own family, then the husband shall feed her with bread made of wheat, and with one or two of the *bajjahs."*[1]

If, on the other hand, it is the husband who is poor, he must feed her with white bread and *bajjahs,* the husband using his best exertions to provide his wife with an agreeable meal,"[2] the balance constituting a debt to the wife, payable when the husband's position has improved. The husband who is in easy circumstances is obliged to provide for and maintain the slaves and personal attendants of his wife, "because he is obliged to provide his wife's maintenance so far as may suffice, and it is not sufficient unless her servants also be supported, they being essential to her ease and comfort."[3] According to Abu Hanifa she is not entitled to maintenance of more than one servant, while

[1] Kazi Khan.
[2] Ibid.
[3] See Hidaya, Bk. IV, Ch. 15. Fet. Abdul Rahim, p. 127, et. seq.

the majority hold that she may have as many as are sufficient to insure to her the same degree of comfort to which she was accustomed in her father's house.[1] But if the servant is not able "to cook or prepare bread, then she is not entitled to maintenance as against the husband of the wife, because, unlike a wife to whom maintenance is due (in consideration of her being detained), a servant is entitled to maintenance solely because of her services, and if she is unable to render any she is not entitled to support.[2]

If the husband "is the master of a good table" he is obliged to maintain the particular slave whom his wife brings along with her. He cannot say "I will not maintain thy servant, but I will give thee one of my own to serve thee," or "I will serve thee myself."

In case the husband has children, and one servant is not enough for their service, the maintenance of two servants or more, as many as may be required for the children, will be due from him.

The maintenance of the servant is of the commonest kind and need not reach in quality the maintenance of the wife. "She (the servant) shall be provided with a shirt and a sheet with which to surround her loins of coarse cloth, and a blanket of the cheapest kind, and a *khoof,* because the servant girl has occasion to go out for her mistress's out-door business . . . and it is not necessary for the wife's servant to be provided with a hairband, because her hair need not be concealed from view."[3]

When the judge has decreed maintenance according to the standard applicable to a poor man, and the husband afterwards becomes rich, the matter may again be made the subject of contest, and the maintenance is to be brought up to "the standard of the wealthy."

[1] Kazi Khan.
[2] Clavel, Droit Musulman, Vol. I, p. 151. Kadri Pasha.
[3] Kazi Khan.

From the day a valid marriage is contracted, the wife is entitled to clothing to the extent of "what is customary." "What is customary" is rather modest among the Arabs, for Kazi Khan says it is fixed at two shirts and two hair-bands, and one sheet every year. "Some have said that the sheet is a covering, which the woman puts on when she is going out; whilst others have said that the sheet means a cloth which is worn in the night; and when Muhammed speaks of 'two shirts' and 'two hair-bands,' he means one for each of the hot and the cold seasons; and what is to be used for the hot season is thin, so as to be fit for the hot season; and what is to be used for the winter is thick, so as to be fit to keep off the cold; and Muhammed has not mentioned the trousers in connection with clothing for the hot weather, but trousers are necessary for cold weather." A husband is not bound to furnish his wife with stockings and embroidered sheets in connection with maintenance; "because these are not necessary except when going out, and it is not necessary for the husband to furnish his wife with means for going out."[1]

Clothing is to be provided twice a year for six months at a time and the wife is not entitled to any more before the expiration of the term. If, then, the dress be torn or lost within the term, and it should appear that this was due to the negligence of the wife, the husband is not liable for another. If, on the other hand, it should appear that the dress was worn in the customary way and suffered only from ordinary wear and tear, she would be entitled to another one. And also if, after the expiration of the period fixed, the garment should still be good, and it should appear that this had happened in consequence of its not having been worn, or worn only part of the time and alternately with other clothes, she would be entitled to another dress.

It is incumbent upon a husband to provide a separate

[1] Ibid.

apartment for his wife, free from the intrusion of his or even her own people without her permission; "because this is essentially necessary to her, and is therefore her due, the same as maintenance; and the word of God appoints her a dwelling house as well as a subsistence; and as it is incumbent upon a husband to provide a habitation for his wife, so is he not at liberty to admit any person to share in it, as this would be injurious to her, by endangering her property and obstructing her enjoyment of his society."

On her side, the wife cannot give lodging to any of her relatives or to her own children by a former marriage. In both cases the consent of the husband is necessary.[1]

But if the place assigned by the husband is a house in which there are several rooms, and he has assigned to her a room which she can lock and unlock at her will, she cannot claim another residence unless the other inmates injure her by acts or by words. But the lodging of a co-wife in the same house gives her a right to demand a separate lodging, "which should have a kitchen and privy," although there is nothing to show that the co-wife does anything to injure her.

"A house which has no neighbors is not a legal house."[2] If the wife suffers from solitude in the house supplied to her by the husband; if it is not inhabited by other tenants and "has such lofty walls that she apprehends harm to her mind from its large dimensions," or if her husband goes out and absents himself at night while she has no servant or child to keep her company, the husband will be required to provide her a companion, or another habitation where she will not have to complain of solitude.

If the wife complains of the husband's annoyances and bad conduct and prays that the husband may be directed to lodge her among good people, who may be able to know

[1] Majma', Vol. I, p. 389.
[2] Al-Nahr.

whether he treats her well or ill, the judge should, if cognizant that the facts are as stated, rebuke the husband and forbid him to maltreat her. If he is not cognizant of the facts, he shall inquire of the neighbors who are respectable about the husband's conduct. But if in the neighborhood there is nobody on whom the judge can rely or if they evidently lean towards the husband, then he shall order the husband to provide for her a residence amongst "virtuous people."

The husband, beyond all that is enumerated, is also bound to supply his wife with tools of grinding and baking, and the utensils of drinking and cooking, as well as all articles of furniture for the house, such as mats, carpets, beds and pillows, and those used in cleaning, such as a comb, oil and alkali or soap, and the perfumery and other things indispensable for the toilet of the wife, in accordance with the custom of the country.[1]

A release of the husband from his obligation of maintenance is void if the judge had not at the time decreed its nature and amount; "because she released him before the obligation came into existence."[2] And if the judge has fixed a certain sum payable monthly or yearly and the wife then releases her claim without any compensation, this release is good only as regards the maintenance for one month, or one year, as the case may be. This is true even though the wife releases in these terms: "Thou art released from my maintenance for ever, as long as I am thy wife." But a man may compound with his wife for her maintenance for a nominal sum. The principle in cases of composition is that (if it be made for something which a judge could lawfully decree immediately as maintenance against the husband), the composition is to be taken as a measure of the maintenance, not as something received in lieu of it,

[1] Bahr.
[2] Kazi Khan.

and that whether the composition have taken place before of the maintenance, not as something taken in lieu of it, A release from arrears of maintenance, however, is valid.

Obligation to maintain ceases with the dissolution of marriage, either by death, by separation, or by any other cause.

II. Duties of the Wife

The wife should be obedient to her husband in so far as his commands are legally allowed and are ordained as duties of marriage. The Koran provides: "The honest women are obedient, careful in the absence of their husbands, for that God preserveth them by committing them to the care and protection of the men."[1] The wife is bound to preserve the husband's property from loss or waste in his absence, not to give away in excess of what is customary and to keep his house in good order. She is not bound, however, to render such personal services as baking bread, cooking food, cleaning the house with a broom, spinning or weaving, unless she cares to. "And the lawyer Abu Leith, on whom be peace, says, if the wife does not cook and prepare bread, then the husband is bound to provide her with cooked victuals only when she is the daughter of respectable persons and did not herself work in her own family."[2] If, on the other hand, she is not "the daughter of respectable persons," she can be forced to do her own cooking and such work as is consistent with her station in society. Charleville contrasts the respective duties of wives under the Hebrew and Muhammedan laws. The Jewish wife, unlike the Arab, was required not only to perform the household duties, but also to do productive work for the

[1] Ch. IV, v. 38.
[2] Kazi Khan.

husband.[1] Even when able to keep many servants, she was not permitted to live in idleness, as "idleness leads to sin."[2] Under the Muhammedan law, on the other hand, the wife may not engage in work without the husband's permission even if the proceeds are destined to enrich the husband.[3]

A woman is legally bound to yield her person to her husband, in so far as this is required at reasonable times and places and with due regard to health and decency. If she denies herself to her husband without a valid cause, she becomes rebellious (*nashizah*). She can refuse herself, however, till the advance dower has been paid. If she has once surrendered and subsequently denies herself in order to obtain payment of her dower, she is not to be deemed rebellious, according to Abu Hanifa; but Abu Yusuf and Imam Muhammed, the two disciples of Hanifa, maintain that, after having once surrendered herself, she has no right to withdraw herself from further connubial intercourse.[4]

The wife may also refuse intercourse with her husband until she has attained puberty. Until then the husband is entitled only to her company. The age of puberty depends upon the constitution and physique of the individual. Multeka says that, in the absence of physical indications, the age of fifteen is to be considered as the age of puberty. The Malikite jurists, on the other hand, fix this age at eighteen.

That a husband does not say his prayers, does not appear to be a sufficient reason for refusing to live with him. As well might a man who is indebted to another refrain from discharging his obligations because his creditor leaves "many rights of God unsatisfied, such as almsgiving

[1] Charleville, Code Rabbinque, Vol. II, p. 73.
[2] For more details see M. Mielziner, Jewish Law of Marriage and Divorce, p. 103; L. G. Levy, La famille dans l'antiquité Israelite.
[3] Eschbach, Droit Musulman, p. 98.
[4] Durr-al-Mukhtar, Fet. Kazi Khan.

(*zakat*), pilgrimage (*hajj*) or the land-tax due to the sovereign (*ushr*)."

A wife is bound to live with her husband and to follow him wherever he desires to go; and if she refuses to do so without valid reason, the courts of justice, on a suit by the husband, will order her to live with him. The wife may not refuse to live with her husband on any of the following grounds:[1]

(1) That her father objects to it.

(2) That she wishes to live near her parents.

(3) That the conjugal domicile chosen by the husband is far from that of her parents.

(4) That she does not want to depart from the city of her birth.

(5) That she has been brought up in a city and does not wish to live in the country.

(6) That the climate of the country which her husband has chosen as their conjugal domicile is likely to be injurious to her health.

(7) That he maltreats her.

(8) That she has an account to settle with her husband.

The house chosen for conjugal domicile, however, must, as has already been stated, be a proper or "legal house." A wife may also refuse to live with the husband on land which he has usurped, "because the woman does what is right by refusing to live in a usurped place, and is not disobedient or rebellious (*nashizah*)."[2]

On the other hand, she cannot refuse to live with her husband on the ground that he resides on royal lands, private property of the sovereign, and lives on the Sultan's

[1] Sautayra, Droit Musulman, p. 199.
[2] Kazi Khan.

charity.[1] It is difficult to see why this question was raised. One theory is that it is not honorable for a respectable man to live on charity. Fetawai Alemkiri[2] says, on the other hand, that it is not lawful for a sovereign to appropriate any more public funds to his use than so much as will enable him and his family to live with comfort, in order that he may avoid temptation regarding his subjects' property. Abu Bakr, the first Khalif and father-in-law of the Prophet, was allowed the modest sum of four hundred *dirhams* per annum, and Ali, his son-in-law fixed for himself five hundred *dirhams* per month. We may infer that what was held to be unlawful for the sovereign to take would be considered unlawful for him to give and, therefore, improper for his subjects to take without payment.

It seems that in every case in which the question of the wife's duty to live with the husband is raised, the decision will depend upon the special features of the case. The general principle of the Muhammedan law on the subject is the same as in other systems of law, *viz.*, that a wife is bound to reside with her husband unless there is some good reason to justify her refusal. This duty is imposed upon her, however, only in the absence of an agreement governing the rights and duties of the spouses. The law recognizes the validity of express stipulations respecting the conjugal domicile. If it be agreed that the husband shall allow his wife to live always with her parents, he cannot afterwards force her to leave her father's house for his own. Such a stipulation, however, in order to be effective must be put in writing, and, if there be a deed of marriage, it must be

[1] If the wife says: "I shall not reside with thee on the royal land is in the husband, and if the woman refuses to live with him she shall be considered disobedient. And verily we have stated before that, if the husband is residing on usurped land and the woman refuses to live with him on such land, she shall not be considered disobedient, and she shall be entitled to separate maintenance from her husband; and the reason of that is, that usurpation is absolutely unlawful, nor is there any doubt regarding the same; contrary to the case of the land of the Sultan and his property." Kazi Khan.

[2] Vol. III, pp. 402 and 403.

entered in the deed. An informal understanding is not sufficient in the eye of the law.

As part of her duty of obedience a wife is bound to remain in her husband's house and not quit it without his permission. Kazi Khan enumerates four cases in which a wife is permitted to go out of the house without the permission of her husband:

(1) When she is in a house which it is feared may come down.

(2) When a particular occasion is afforded her to attend a meeting of learning and to inform herself of rules of practice relating to prayer and purification, provided always that her husband is not sufficiently versed in learning. If her husband is learned in the law and he informs her accordingly, then she is not entitled to go out of the house without his permission. And even if the husband himself is ignorant but obtains the answer from a learned man, she is not entitled to go out; but if the husband who is himself ignorant refrains from questioning a learned man, then she is entitled to go out of the house without his permission, in order to satisfy herself on the particular point of law, "because the acquisition of knowledge and information, in matters in which there is need of knowledge, is a binding duty on every Muslim, male or female, and, therefore, such acquisition shall override the rights of the husband."

(3) When she finds opportunity to make an indispensable pilgrimage, in the company of a relative whom it is unlawful for her to marry.

(4) It is permitted her to visit her parents when they are in affliction or in ill health, and also to see such of her relatives as are within the forbidden degrees of marriage. Filial duty may require that she visit her parents; if, for example, her father is suffering from a protracted illness and has no one to tend him, she may visit him with-

out her husband's consent and may remain with him in order to afford him the necessary attention;[1] and if under such circumstances the husband forbids her to visit her father, "it is open to her to disobey her husband and be submissive to her father, whether her father is a Muslim or an infidel; because it is obligatory on her to remain fixed in her submission and offer of help to her parents and, therefore, such submission shall have preference over the rights of her husband."[2]

Besides the above enumerated four cases, some authorities have held that a wife is entitled to visit her relatives within the prohibitive degrees once a month or (according to others) once a year, without the permission of her husband. But under no circumstances can she spend the night at their house.[3]

The wife cannot go out of the house for any other reason without her husband's express permission. If, for example, she is a midwife, or a "washer of the dead,"[4] and wishes to go out in order to discharge the duties in which she is versed, or to attend to any other business, she must first obtain her husband's permission.

III. Marital Authority

In the discussion of dower and maintenance it has already been pointed out that there is an absolute separation of property between wife and husband. The married woman keeps her own property, including the dower; she can dispose of all or of part of it without the permission

[1] Fet. Abdul Rahim.
[2] Kazi Khan.
[3] Fet. Abdul Rahim.
[4] In Muhammedan countries it is customary to wash the dead before burial, and women are invariably washed by female "washers of the dead."

or consent of her husband; his marital power gives him no right to oppose her in such matters. She may herself receive the rent and revenue of her property or may appoint another person than her husband to administer it for her. The contracts and agreements made by a married woman are valid without the authorization or ratification of her husband. A transaction between the spouses, such as a sale of land or of a house[1] or of any other property, is perfectly valid.

Whatever fortune she may possess, the wife is not bound to contribute anything toward the household expenses. She is not even bound to contribute to her own personal needs, when the satisfaction of these needs forms part of the husband's duty of maintenance.

In this regular and invariable separation of the wife's property from that of the husband the Muhammedan law differs from the western systems of jurisprudence. In the legislation of the other states of continental Europe separation is at best facultative and must be established by antenuptial agreement. In the countries governed by English law it is a recent innovation, and it is not yet universally established. The difference is a logical outcome of the respective positions of women in Eastern and Western countries. The Muhammedan woman is far from being the equal of her spouse; the Koran says that "men shall have the pre-eminence above women, because of all the advantages wherein God hath caused the one of them to excel the other;[2] they are superior in understanding and strength, and enjoy privileges and dignities in church and state, go to war in defence of God's true religion, and claim a double share of their deceased ancestor's estate.[3] Connected with this inequality is the fact that the power of

[1] The Ottoman Land Code; trans. F. Ongley, pp. 226 and 227.
[2] Ch. IV, v. 38.
[3] Ferruh Effendi, Mevakib, p. 145.

the husband to divorce his wife is, as we shall see later, almost unlimited. In view of these facts, particularly the husband's power of divorce, a separation of property seems to be necessary in order to protect women and their property from the absolute domination of the husband.

The legal personality of the wife is not merged under the Muhammedan law in that of her husband, as in the English law, nor does her property *ipso facto* become his. Each keeps his or her own distinct personality, and their control over their property is not in any degree impaired by the union. Not only do the paraphernalia, which a bride brings with her from her father's home, remain her absolute property, but the marriage outfit provided by the bridegroom becomes likewise her exclusive property.

The property rights of the married parties always remain distinct. Originally, at the commencement of the married life, it is easy to distinguish between the goods which belong exclusively to the wife and those which belong to the husband. Later, after the husband and the wife have lived together for a considerable time, it becomes difficult as a matter of fact to distinguish the property of the one from the property of the other. Should a dispute arise between the parties, or, after their decease, between their respective heirs, regarding household effects, then, in the absence of any direct proof, the presumption of law is that the "things which by custom appertain to women" are the wife's property and those "which appertain to men" are the husband's, while everything which is regarded as having been necessary or useful to the joint establishment belongs to the survivor.[1]

The power of the husband over his wife, accordingly, is only disciplinary. He has a right to deprive a disobedient wife of her liberty and to inflict on her moderate personal chastisement. The Koran says "those whose perverseness

[1] Seyid Amir Ali, Muhammedan Law, Vol. I, pp. 406 and 407.

ye fear, admonish them and remove them into bed-chambers and beat them; but if they submit to you, then do not seek a way against them" (*i. e.*, take no further measures against them).

According to Kazi Khan a husband is entitled to inflict corporal chastisement on his wife for four reasons. "First, if the wife gives up beautifying or adorning herself (*i. e.*, if she neglects her toilet), when the husband desires her to beautify herself. Second, if she refuses compliance with his wishes, when he is inclined to have intercourse with her, she being pure. Third, if she does not observe her prayers; but, according to some traditions from Muhammed, on whom be peace, it is not his right to inflict corporal chastisement on her for refraining to observe her prayers; and to refrain from bathing and purifying herself after she has become impure is tantamount to refraining from her prayers. Fourth, if the wife goes out of his house without his permission, after she has received her advance dower in full."

This marital power of correction, as is the case in the English common law, has never been expressly taken away from the husband, but at the present time it is highly improbable that he could inflict any personal injuries on his wife without subjecting himself to criminal liability. The most a husband can do, when his wife commits a fault for which the law has no judicial penalty, is to punish her in moderation. He would not be allowed to use violence towards her even under extreme provocation.[1]

The following passage from the opinion of Judge Mahmoud in the case of Abdul Kadir v. Salima is an illustration of the position of modern Muhammedan jurists on the subject: "This conception of the mutual rights and obligations arising from marriage between the husband and wife, bears in all main features close similarity to the Roman law and other European systems which are derived from

[1] Clavel, Droit Musulman, p. 164.

that law; and even regarding the power of correction the English law seems to resemble the Muhammedan, for even under the former 'the old authorities say the husband may beat his wife'; and if in modern times the rigour of the law has been mitigated, it is because in England, as in this country, the criminal law has stepped in to give the wife personal security, which the matrimonial law does not. The Muhammedan law, on a question of what is legal cruelty between man and wife, would not differ materially from the English law."[1] In 1865 the court of Algeria held the husband liable for inflicting personal injuries on his wife and granted her a divorce, although it appeared that the wife had committed adultery.[2] The same rule would probably be applied in Turkey, in Egypt, or in any other Muhammedan country that is influenced by the Western systems of jurisprudence.

The power of a husband over his wife has been indicated in the sections on rights and duties of the respective parties, but it seems desirable to summarize what has already been said and to add further details. The husband, after payment to the wife of the part of the dower payable in advance, has the right to forbid her to leave his house without his permission, except in the cases in which she is allowed to do so, *viz.*, to visit her parents once a week and her relations within the prohibitive degrees once a year. He may also forbid her, even when accompanied by her relatives, to visit and mix with "foreign women" or to attend festivals and entertainments, especially "on occasions of misfortune to others."[3] He may compel her to leave her father's house, when she is not too young, and to live among respectable neighbors in any quarter of the town. He may prevent her relatives from staying with her in his house,

[1] I. R. L., 8 All., 149 F. B. (1886).
[2] Clavel, Droit Musulman, Vol. I, p. 164.
[3] Kazi Khan.

whether the house is his property or leased to him.[1] There is some difference of opinion as to how far a husband can prevent his wife's parents and relatives from entering his house to visit her, but "according to our *sheikhs* (Hanifite) he cannot prevent her parents from visiting her in his house on Fridays, though he may forbid their remaining with her; and the *fetwa* agrees with this. In like manner, he cannot prevent her from going out to visit them once every Friday, the *fetwa* being in accordance with this also. But may he prevent other persons than her parents from visiting her? Some say that he cannot prevent those within the prohibitive degrees from visiting her once a month, but according to the *sheikhs* of Balkh and the *fetwa*, she is entitled to receive such visits only once in the year; and the rule is the same, with the same difference of opinion, as to her going out to visit her relatives within the prohibitive degrees, such as her uncles maternal or paternal and her brothers." But a husband cannot prevent her parents or her child by another husband from seeing and conversing with her at any time.[2]

The husband is entitled to prevent his wife from "indulging in poetry, *i. e.*, in chanting musical songs;"[3] and as part of his duty to her he may compel her to "say her prayers." There is some doubt as to what measures a husband may take to force his wife to "say her prayers." Some have gone so far as to allow him to beat her; others deny this; but his right to divorce her has not been questioned. And this he may do although he may not have sufficient means to pay her dower. "It is reported of Abu Hafs of Bukhara that he said that 'seeing God with the liability of the wife's dower on his shoulders is more agreeable to

[1] Radd-al-Mukhtar, Vol. VIII, pp. 390 et seq. Clavel, Droit Musulman, Vol. I, p. 170.

[2] Kazi Khan. Sautayra, Droit Musulman, Vol. I, p. 195. Clavel, Droit Musulman, Vol. I, p. 164. Kadri Pasha, pp. 52 and 53.

[3] Kazi Khan.

me than that the husband should have intercourse with a wife who does not say her prayers.' "[1]

The question how far a wife is compelled to cook or to do other household work has been discussed in the section on the duties of the wife. A wife who may legally be compelled to cook may not refuse to do so on the ground that her husband is a wicked man. So if "a wicked man invites wicked men, it is proper for his wife to bake bread and to cook food, but she shall, when baking the bread and cooking the food, form an intention that so long as they shall occupy themselves in eating they shall refrain from drinking wine, just as, when a man sits in the company of wicked persons, with the intention formed in his mind that they shall refrain from their wickedness for the period he shall be sitting with them, it is allowable to him to sit with them, and he shall be rewarded for this. God knows best!"[2]

In case of disaccord between the parties, the judge before whom they bring their complaints may refer the case to two upright arbitrators, preferably one from the husband's family and one from the wife's; and the arbitrators after hearing both sides shall seek to effect a reconciliation; "because a bad temper often makes its appearance between the married couple, and to punish for it the first time is to engender an illfeeling between them; accordingly the judge should first confine himself to an injunction; perhaps their dispute will be reconciled, and it often happens that each of them is at fault."[3] If the attempt at reconciliation is fruitless, the arbitrators may grant a divorce when empowered to do so by both parties.

If the woman complains to the court of the bad treatment of her husband, and brings positive proof of his having used violence towards her, even though under provocation, he will be punished.

[1] Kazi Khan.
[2] Kazi Khan.
[3] Al-Nahr.

PART III

DIVORCE

In every legal system which places the wife under the authority of the husband, the power of divorce was regarded at the outset as a natural corollary to the marital rights. Among the early Arabs the husband[1] could exercise this power without any restriction. As among other primitive peoples, it was a right to abandon rather than to divorce in the legal sense. The legislation of Muhammed, limiting the power of the husband to divorce his wife, marked a departure from the ancient customs of the Arabs. Muhammed, however, is said to have borrowed the doctrines of the Jews, who, while upholding the marital right of divorce, imposed certain restrictions on its exercise.

A careful study of the legislation of Muhammed on divorce and of the traditions that perpetuated his views on this subject will make it apparent that the Prophet, if not willing to prohibit divorce altogether, was desirous of restricting it to the limits which are recognized by modern legal systems. He said that of all lawful things the most hateful in the sight of God is divorce, because it puts an end to marriage, which it is the object of the lawgiver to

[1] Perron, in his Femmes Arabes, says that in some cases women of the higher classes would, before marriage, reserve to themselves the power of divorcing the husband, and when they made up their mind to do so they signified their intention by changing the position of their tents, which meant a repudiation of the marriage. This appears to be a survival from an earlier type of marriage, in which the husband did not acquire full marital authority. Cf. Lamnens, Berceau de L'Islam, p. 282.

encourage. It is indeed valid, without any reason assigned; but in the absence of necessity it is condemned. Abu Hanifa has declared divorce forbidden, unless there is need for it. Divorce without need is an act of folly, an abuse of discretion and sheer ingratitude for a blessing; it is simply an act intended to annoy the wife, her people and her children. There is need of divorce when there is incompatibility of tempers, and particularly when there is settled aversion, which necessarily leads to the nonobservance of the ordinances of the Almighty. But when there is an absence of necessity, divorce is, in principle, prohibited. The Almighty had therefore said: "If they (women) obey you, do not seek an occasion for troubling them," that is, do not seek an occasion for separation.[1] It remains to be seen how far the Prophet was able to give effect to his moral views in his legislation.

The contract of marriage, under the Muhammedan law, may be dissolved in three ways:

(1) By the husband, at his will and without the intervention of any court of law.

(2) By mutual consent of the husband and wife, without the intervention of any court of law.

(3) By a judicial decree, on the application of the husband or of the wife.

I. Repudiation by the Husband (Talak)

Dissolution of marriage by the husband, at his will, without the intervention of any court of law, is called *talak,* which literally means the unmaking or untying of a knot. In the legal sense, it signifies a release from the marriage tie.[2] This one-sided power of divorce is exclusively

[1] Al-Nahr, Radd-al-Mukhtar.
[2] Khulasat-al-Mukhtarin, pp. 86, 87.

in the hand of the husband, unless in the marriage contract he has expressly given a similar power to the wife.

In order that repudiation by the husband be effective, it is essential that he should have attained majority, that he should be in his right mind, and that he should be awake, divorce pronounced by a sleepwalker being of no effect. As to whether he must act of his own free will, and must have a serious intention to dissolve the marriage tie, there is a difference of opinion.

The answer of Hanifa to the first question is in the affirmative: a divorce pronounced under duress is effective. Against this view there is a formidable array of juristic opinions. Among the dissenters is Shafi'i, who declares that a person who is compelled has no option, and no formal act of law is worthy of regard unless it be purely optional. To this the Hanifite jurists answer in a manner which is characteristic of their age. They argue that voluntary divorce is motived by "necessity," namely, the necessity of separation from a wife who is disagreeable to the husband, and that divorce made under duress is likewise motived by necessity, namely, the necessity of escaping the evils with which one is threatened by the person exercising duress. The real basis of this reasoning is the fact, which was recognied by Roman jurists also, that the man who acts under intimidation has a choice between two evils, namely, that with which he is threatened and that which he is called upon to do; that in acting under duress he makes such a choice; and that to make choice is an act of volition. The Roman law, however, treated the act under duress as void because the person so acting does not desire the effect of his act,[1] and has been actuated in his choice by methods which the law does not sanction.

Repudiation by a drunken man is held to be effective, although it is difficult to see by what process of reasoning the drunken man is distinguished from the somnambulist.

[1] Cf. Hidaya, Bk. IV, Ch. I.

A distinction is made, however, between cases of drunkenness; and it is maintained that if a man was compelled to drink against his will and pronounced a divorce in a state of intoxication, the divorce is not effective. This distinction is accepted, singularly enough, by those who hold that repudiation under duress is effective.

There is no consensus of opinion regarding the effect of a divorce pronounced in jest, but the weight of opinion is that it is effective. Muhammed declared that in three things, marriage, vows and divorce, jesting is not permitted. It was doubtless his meaning that men should not trifle with matters of such solemnity, but his utterance is interpreted to mean that both marriage and divorce made in jest are valid and effective. In this instance a literal interpretation of the Prophet's words leads to results directly opposed to his legislative policy. In view of the validity of repudiation pronounced in jest, it is not surprising that a repudiation is effective even when there has been a mistake. "If a person meaning to say 'Zeinab, thou art repudiated,' should by a slip of the tongue say 'Amrut' instead, the person actually named would be repudiated."[1]

Repudiation (*talak*) may be express (*sarih*) or implied (*kinayah*). The use of the word *talak* in all its grammatical forms is almost always taken to signify express repudiation, although other words may be similarly construed. If the husband uses the word *talak,* the marriage is repudiated, and a plea that he meant something else than divorce, is not to be admitted in court, "though it is different as between him and his God." As to the wife, she may not lawfully admit her husband to her embraces when she has heard the words herself or when they have been communicated to her by a trustworthy witness.

[1] Baillie, Vol. I, p. 208.

The jurists recognize a great number of formulae by which repudiation may be effected, some obvious in their significance, others conveying their meaning by implication. To consider these in detail would uselessly lengthen this treatise. I select a few typical forms, some of them metaphorical or allusive. "I am forbidden to thee," "Count,"[1] "You are cut off," "The reins are thrown upon your neck," "Veil yourself," "Seek for a mate," *etc.*

Repudiation does not necessarily or normally dissolve marriage at once, without opportunity for reflection and reconsideration. According to the greater or less delay involved, the jurists distinguish three forms or modes of repudiation: (1) *Ahsan,* or very laudable divorce; (2) *Hasan,* or laudable divorce; and (3) *Bid'i,* a heretical form of divorce. The first and the second forms are known as exemplary (*talak-al-Sunnah*).

(1) *Ahsan* is effected by a single declaration of repudiation, which must be made to the wife during a "clean period" (*tuhr*), *i. e.,* between menses, and by subsequent abstention from intercourse with her during the customary period of probation (*iddah*).

Until this period has elapsed, the repudiation is revocable (*riji*), and the husband may resume conjugal relations with his wife, if he be so inclined, by a revocation of the repudiation. This he can do whether she be willing or not, according to the Koran, "Hold them with humanity," in which there is no distinction between willingness and unwillingness on the part of the wife.[2] The husband may signify his intention to reestablish the conjugal relation either by speech or by conduct. To retain the wife by speech (*i. e.,* by express revocation of the repudiation), is commendable; to retain her by conduct is abominable, yet

[1] Count here refers to the number of repudiations; *cf. infra.*
[2] Kifaya, Vol. II, p. 248.

legally valid.[1] Retention on the part of an insane person, however, may be effected only by an act or conduct. Retention is valid though made under compulsion or in jest or by mistake.

Until the period of probation has expired, the marriage tie is not dissolved. The husband retains marital authority over the wife; and if during this period of probation either party dies, the other may inherit.[2] The right to revoke a repudiation before the period of probation has elapsed exists only in the case of marriages which have been consummated. Repudiation of a wife with whom marriage has not been consummated is irrevocable.

After the expiration of the period of probation the repudiation becomes definite and absolute (*ba'in*), and matrimonial relations may again be established only after a new contract has been entered into and dissolved.[3]

(2) *Hasan*. A less laudable but approved method of divorce is effected by three repudiations in three successive "clean periods" (*tuhrs*); or, in case the menstrual courses are suspended, owing to pregnancy or any other cause, by three repudiations in three successive months. After the first and the second repudiation, the situation is the same as in the *ahsan* form of divorce; that is, the repudiation is revocable. It becomes absolute when the third repudiation has been pronounced, or when the period of probation (*iddah*) has expired without revocation of repudiation, by express words or by conduct.

In the case of a slave wife, two successive repudiations have the same effect as three repudiations in the case of the free wife.

The distinguishing feature of this method of divorce is

[1] Mahmud Essad, pp. 169, 170.
[2] Kifaya, Vol. II, p. 248. Al-Nahr. Abdul Kadir, p. 296.
[3] Fetawai Feizié, pp. 106, 107.

that remarriage between the divorced parties is permissible only when the divorced woman has contracted another marriage and this marriage has been dissolved.

Primitive and even absurd as the foregoing rule may seem, it is defended by many modern writers. This check was certainly intended to control a jealous and sensitive but half-cultured race, by appealing to the sense of honor;[1] and it undoubtedly operates to lessen the frequency of divorce.

(3) *Bid'i*—a form of divorce which is not approved and which is regarded as heretical—is effected by three repudiations, which may be pronounced at any time (not merely in "clean periods") and without definite intervals. Although this method of divorce is regarded by Muhammedan lawyers as irregular and sinful, it is nevertheless recognized as effective; and it produces precisely the same results which attach to the *hasan* form. It does not appear to have been recognized by the Prophet; on the contrary, it is said that he strongly disapproved it. It is reported that on a certain occasion, when news was brought to him that one of his disciples had divorced his wife, pronouncing the three repudiations (*talaks*) at one and the same time, "the Prophet stood up in anger on his carpet and declared that the man was making a plaything of the words of God and made him take back his wife."[2]

This form of divorce was legitimatized in the second century of the Muhammedan era, when the Omeyad tyrants, finding the checks imposed by the Prophet on the facility of repudiation galling, looked about for some escape from the strictness of the law, and found it in the pliability of the jurists.[3]

Whether a repudiation is to be regarded as triple, so

[1] See Sédillot, Histories des Arabes.
[2] Radd-al-Mukhtar, Vol. II, p. 634.
[3] Sayed Amir Ali, Muhammedan Law, Vol. II, pp. 411, 412.

that it becomes illegal for the parties to remarry before the intervention of a marriage between the wife and a third person, depends upon the words employed. Here again the jurists find opportunity for over literal or over subtle interpretation of words and phrases. A few examples will suffice. If a màn says to his wife: "You are divorced," or "Be separated," there is but one repudiation. If he says: "Thou are repudiated and I have repudiated thee," two repudiations take place; "and though he should say: 'I intended by the second expression only corroboration of the fact,' no credit could be given to his allegation in law, though it would be good as a matter between him and his conscience."

If a woman says to her husband: "Repudiate me and repudiate me and repudiate me," and the husband answers: "I have repudiated thee," this amounts to a triple repudiation, whether the man so meant it or not. But if the wife had said: "Repudiate me, repudiate me, repudiate me," without the conjunction "and," and the husband had answered: "I have repudiated thee," it would be open to him to explain whether he meant one or three repudiations.

If a man informs his wife that her trunk or her neck or half of her is divorced, a repudiation takes place. But "if the husband says to his wife: 'Your hand' or 'your foot is divorced,' there is no repudiation. Zufer and Shafi'i maintain the contrary."[1]

If a man says: "You are divorced from this place to Syria," there is but one repudiation; although Zufer, a disciple of Hanifa, thinks the result a triple divorce "because he thus gives the repudiation a description of length."[2]

Repudiation may be conditional; that is, its effect may be made to depend upon a future act or event.[3] If the hus-

[1] Hidaya, Bk. IV, Ch. 2.
[2] Hidaya, Bk. IV, Ch. 2.
[3] Inayah, Vol. II, p. 140, *et seq.* Mahmud Essad, Kitab-i-nikah, pp. 154, 155.

band says to his wife: "You are under divorce in Mecca," repudiation takes place at once and in every country; but if he were to say: "You are under divorce when you enter Mecca," there is no repudiation until she enters Mecca.

If a man says to his wife: "As often as you repeat a good sentence, you are repudiated," and she says: "Praise be to God and there is no God but God and God is most great," only one repudiation takes place; but if she were to repeat the same sentences without the connective "and," there would be a triple repudiation.

Repudiation may be effected by writing as validly as by words; but repudiation by signs or gestures is ineffective, unless the husband is dumb. In that case, if his gestures or signs are intelligible, there is a valid repudiation.

Repudiation by a sick man is of no effect if the husband dies before the wife's period of probation or *iddah* is over, or, in the *hasan* form of divorce, before the third repudiation is pronounced. In such cases the wife is entitled to inherit from the estate of her deceased husband, irrespective of the repudiation. This rule is accepted only by the Hanifites; Shafi'ites maintain, on the contrary, that at least in the *hasan* form of divorce repudiation is effective and the woman is barred from inheritance.

What is meant by sickness is not very clear. Baillie says: "When a man is unable to go out of his home for necessary avocations he is sick, whether he can stand up in the house or not." Hidaya speaks of the husband being on his "death bed," but does not define just what sickness in the legal sense means. This author says that, if a husband besieged in a town repudiate his wife, she does not inherit, but that if a man engaged in fighting or a criminal being carried to execution were to repudiate his wife, she would inherit; "for it is a rule that the wife of the evader inherits of him. The husband has to be sick from a dangerous illness or to be in such a situation as affords room to apprehend his death . . . but a man who is besieged in a town cannot be said to be in any imminent danger."[1] Kazi Khan says a man is sick only when he is bedridden and can not manage his affairs; and Fetawai Alemkiri defines the sickness to be taken into account as "one which it is highly probable will issue fatally; in the case of a man it disables him from getting up for necessary avocations out of his house, for instance, when he is a merchant, from going to his shop." Fetawai Ali Effendi speaks of "death sickness," but no satisfactory definition is given.[2]

Perhaps the most satisfactory definition is given by an English judge.[3]

"My examination of the authorities leads me to the conclusion that, in order to establish *marz-ul-maut* (death sickness), there must be present at least three conditions:

(a) Proximate danger of death, so that there is, as it is phrased, a preponderance of apprehension, that is, that at the given time death must be more probable than life.

(b) There must be some degree of subjective apprehension of death in the mind of the sick person.

(c) There must be some external *indicia,* chief among which I would place the inability to attend to ordinary avocations."

It is necessary, also, that the sickness which has caused the husband's death be the same as that during which the repudiation was pronounced. So if a man, who has repudiated his wife during an illness subsequently recovers, and then dies from some other cause, the repudiation is valid and the wife does not inherit.[4]

If the husband has repudiated his wife at her own request, then, although he were seriously ill at the time and

[1] Hidaya.

[2] Pp. 90 and 91.

[3] Bachelor, J., in the case of Sarabai v. Rahiabi, I. L. R., 3p Bom. 537 (1905).

[4] Fetawai Ali Effendi, p. 90.

has died before the repudiation has ceased to be revocable, the divorce is effective and the wife has no right of inheritance. Nor will the wife inherit if the repudiation were made dependent on a certain contingency and that contingency occurs at the time when the husband is sick; so, for example, if a husband says: "When you enter this house," or "When such a one repeats evening prayers, you are divorced;" and the condition is fulfilled at a time the husband is sick. In this case the repudiation is held to have been made at the time when it was pronounced, not at the time when it becomes effective.

Agency in Repudiation

Just as a husband may in person repudiate his wife, so he may confer a power of repudiation on a third person, or even upon his wife; and a divorce will take effect if and when the power so conferred is exercised.

This delegation of power is called *tafwiz*. The extent to which marriage and divorce were regarded as ordinary transactions is shown by the fact that serious question arose as to the power of a general agent, appointed to manage all the affairs of the principal, to take charge of his matrimonial relations. Such a general agent, thinking that it will be to the best interest of his principal to get rid of a wife, repudiates her. We are told by Baillie "that authorities differ with regard to such a repudiation, but the correct opinion is that it is not valid. But if the words of appointment were: 'I have made you my agent in all my affairs in which agency is lawful,' the power would be general for sales, marriages and everything else."[1] There is an intimation that even an unauthorized agent may repudiate the wife of an absent principal and that such a repudiation will be effective if ratified by the husband.[2]

[1] Baillie, Vol. I, p. 257.
[2] Fetawai Ali Effendi, p. 73.

A peculiar instance of the delegation of the power of repudiation to a third person is the authorization given to a creditor to repudiate the debtor's wife in the event of the debt remaining unpaid. "When a creditor has said to his debtor: 'If you do not pay me my debt in a month the business of your wife will be in my hands,' and he has replied: 'Let it be so,' and the condition is fulfilled, the creditor may repudiate her."[1] It is interesting to note that this, in effect, is a pledge or mortgage of the wife, or at least of the husband's marital authority, as a security for money borrowed or any other obligation incurred. Since the power to repudiate given to the third person is irrevocable until the period for which it is given has elapsed, the creditor receives a very effective means of compelling payment of the debt, in the power given him to break up his debtor's household.

Delegation to the wife of the power to repudiate, according to legal writers, takes one of three forms: (1) *Ikhtiyar,* giving the wife authority to divorce herself; (2) *Amr-bil-yad,* leaving the matter in her own hands; or (3) *Mashi'ah,* giving her the option to do as she pleases. After close study of the subject, I have not been able to understand these distinctions. There seems to be no difference between *amr-bil-yad,* leaving the matter in her own hands, and *mashi'ah,* giving her the option to do as she pleases; nor is the difference between *ikhtiyar* and *mashi'ah* very clear. For example: if the husband says to his wife: "Choose" or "Repudiate thyself," the jurists treat this authorization as a case of *ikhtiyar;* but authority to "choose" her course of actions seems clearly a case of *mashi'ah.*

All the three classes of cases, when analyzed, appear to resolve themselves into one, *viz.,* cases in which the wife is authorized, if she sees fit, to bring about a repudiation.

In the absence of evidence that the delegation of power

[1] Baillie, Vol. I, p. 251.

was meant to cover a triple repudiation, *i. e.*, an absolute divorce, it is presumed not to extend beyond a repudiation revocable by the husband.

Power delegated to the wife must be exercised at the sitting at which it is given. "If she should rise from the sitting, or betake herself some other employment, recognized as cutting off what has preceded, as, for instance, if she should ask for something to eat, or fall asleep, or remove from the place, or wash or stain her hands or nails, or have to do matrimonially with her husband, or address another man with regard to sale or purchase, all these cancel her option."[1] But so long as she remains at the meeting, though she should prolong it for a day or more by not rising from it, she may repudiate herself.[2]

According to the Hanifites, the power once given cannot be withdrawn. This appears to mean only that words of withdrawal are ineffective; for if, after the husband has given the wife this power and before she exercises it, he takes her by the hand and raises her up, the option is at an end by the termination of the sitting, although this may be against the will of the wife.

Option to repudiate at the same sitting must be distinguished from an antenuptial agreement, by which the wife is permitted to divorce herself in certain contingencies. Such an agreement is valid if the contingencies specified are such as to render her exercise of the power reasonable. Thus the husband may authorize the wife to repudiate herself in case he absents himself from home for a certain period, or maltreats her, or marries a second wife, or does not keep his promise to provide her with clothes of good quality. In these cases the wife must show that the contingency on which she was authorized to dissolve the marriage his arisen. If a man says to his wife: "If I beat

[1] Baillie, Vol. I, p. 239.
[2] Ibid, p. 238.

thee without a fault, thy business is in thy hand," and if she abuses him, or seizes his beard, or says to him: 'O ass!' or 'O fool' or 'God bring you to death,' these are faults"[1] which merit chastisement, and no power vests in the beaten wife to repudiate the marriage.

II. Separation by Mutual Concent (Khul')

Literally, *Khul'* means to strip off, to put off;[2] legally it signifies a separation with the consent and at the instance of the wife, in which she gives or agrees to give a consideration to the husband for the release of the marriage tie. The word "likens the separation of the husband and wife to the act of stripping off clothes, because each of the married couple is like a garment to the other, as the Almighty God hath said: 'They (women) are a garment to you and you are a garment to them,' because each of them screens the condition of his friend and prevents him from doing impure things."[3] God has sanctioned *khul'* by the following passage: "Give the women their dower freely, but if they remit of their own will any part of it, enjoy it with a good grace and pleasure."[4]

When there is a disagreement between husband and wife, and they are both apprehensive that they cannot discharge the duties imposed on them by the marriage relationship, the wife may release herself from the tie by offering the husband a compensation, in consideration of the husband's giving her a *khul'*.

The difference between a divorce by *khul'* and the ordinary marital repudiation is that in *khul'* a single irreversible divorce (*talak-al-bain*) takes place whether the wife's

[1] Baillie, Vol. I, p. 253.
[2] Kifayah, Vol. II, p. 278.
[3] Al-Nahr, p. 302.
[4] Ch. IV, v. 127.

iddah or period of probation is over or not; while in the case of an ordinary repudiation, as we have seen, the husband may revoke the repudiation and re-establish the matrimonial relationship before the period of probation has expired.

Khul' is not valid unless the husband is able to repudiate his wife;[1] that is, he must have reached his majority and be in full possession of his mental faculties. Like the ordinary divorce by repudiation, *khul'* may be effected through agents, and, if the principals are competent, a youth, a madman or a slave may lawfully be appointed by either of them to give or receive the *khul'* in their stead. If the husband is intoxicated, *khul'* will nevertheless be valid.[2]

If *khul'* has been entered into under duress exercised by the wife over the husband, the divorce is valid and the payment of the compensation becomes obligatory on the wife. If, on the other hand, the arrangement has been entered into under coercion exercised by the husband, the divorce is valid, but the agreement of the wife to pay a compensation is not binding; because while a divorce under duress is effective, an obligation incurred under compulsion is null and void.[3]

Khul' is a right which belongs to the parties themselves. Consent of guardians is not necessary, even when the parties are not able to contract a valid marriage without such consent. But fathers may enter into an arrangement of *khul'* on behalf of minor sons or daughters, and if these consent to it, or ratify it, it becomes binding on them.

Khul', like other agreements, is effected by offer and acceptance, at the instance of either of the parties.[4] Hidaya however, says that offer must be made by the wife. If it

[1] Mahmoud Esaad, p. 180.
[2] Baillie, Vol. I, p. 321.
[3] Mahmoud Esaad.
[4] Mahmoud Esaad, p. 179.

is made by the husband to the wife, "it would be abominable in him to take anything from her, because the sacred text says: 'If ye be desirous of changing (that is, repudiating one wife, and marrying another), take not from her anything'; and also because a man, by divorcing his wife from such a desire of change, involves her in distress, and it behooves him not to increase that distress by taking her property."[1]

If the offer is made by the husband, it is even more abominable for him to take more than he has given or settled upon the wife, namely, her dower. But this is a matter of conscience, and if he takes more, and if the repudiation is formally a *khul'* divorce, the arrangement is legally valid. There are some who maintain that the husband may not lawfully take more than the dower he has given his wife, and that, if he does, she has the right to demand restitution of what she has given. The Jami-al-Saghir relates the following story in support of this view. A woman having mentioned her hatred of her husband, he (the Prophet) advised her to give up her dower, as a compensation, to induce the husband to divorce her; to which she replied: "I will give that and more"; but the Prophet answered: "Not more."

No particular words need be used in effecting a *khul'*, according to Hanifites, and the Hidaya goes so far as to say that the mention of a compensation is conclusive evidence of intention.[2] In Shia law, however, "a *khul'* must be pronounced in sacramental terms, the *Sigha* (grammatical form) being as necessary in *khul'* as in *talak*."[3] Hanifites may use such words as sale and purchase as well as *mukhal'e'a* and *khul'*.[4] So if the wife says: "In consideration of my dower, I have bought myself from you," and the

[1] Bk. IV, Ch. 8.
[2] Bk. IV, Ch. 8.
[3] Seyid Amir Ali, p. 442.
[4] Mahmoud Esaad, p. 179.

husband answers: "I have sold you" or "I accept," the *khul' is* validly contracted. If the wife says to her husband: "Give me a *khul'* for a thousand *dirhams,*" and he replies: "Thou art repudiated," there is a difference of opinion as to whether a *khul'* or a repudiation takes place. The weight of opinion is that in such cases of ambiguity the reply is open to explanation by the husband.

In *khul'*, anything that is property (*mal*) may be given in exchange for the divorce: and the rules that apply to dower (*mahr*) are applicable here also. The most common arrangement is a release of the dower, where this has not yet been paid by the husband. This is commonly known as *mubarah* or a mutual release. It extinguishes not only the wife's claim to dower, but also all other rights that either party has acquired through marriage. It does not affect claims that are in no way connected with the marital relationship. So if the husband "claims a certain quantity of cotton (deposited) with her, the claim shall be admissible, because the release is connected solely with the rights of marriage. But the maintenance during *iddah* shall not be revoked unless this be expressly stipulated,[1] nor shall the right to lodging during *iddah* be barred, since this is a requirement of the law."[2]

Instead of releasing her claim to dower or returning the dower received, the wife may pay any sum agreed upon. This may be more or less than the dower; and although, as we have seen, it is contrary to good morals that the husband shall take more than the dower, in strict law he may do so.

When the amount to be paid is not clearly stated, there is room for casuistry. "If a woman says to her husband: 'Grant me *khul'* for what is in my hand,' and he agrees, and it afterwards appears that she had nothing in her hand,

[1] Fetawai Ali Effendi, p. 95.
[2] Al-Nahr Kadir, pp. 305 and 306.

divorce nevertheless takes place, and no further liability rests upon the woman, since she has not deceived her husband by any specific mention of property. But if she were to say: 'Grant me *khul'* for the property in my hand, and he should agree, and it should appear that she had nothing in her hand, she must in this case release to him her claim for dower, because she has deceived him by a specification of property which did not exist; and hence he does not appear to have consented to relinquish his marital right without a return; and the woman cannot be legally bound to give the (non-existent) property, or its value . . . neither can she be laid under any obligation to render the estimated value of her person . . . it is, therefore, established that she remains liable for whatever the husband may have given in consideration of obtaining marital right."[1]

If a woman says to her husband: "Grant me *khul'* for the *dirhams* in my hand, and he agrees, and it then appears that she had nothing in her hand, she is bound to give him three *dirhams*.[2]

Failure on the wife's part to pay the consideration agreed upon in a *khul'* divorce does not invalidate the divorce, so as to enable the husband to sue for a restitution of conjugal rights. It entitles him only to sue for any money or property due under the agreement. If the wife has not released her dower, her failure to pay the consideration agreed upon may of course be used as a defense against her claim for dower. This at least is the majority view; but some hold that the payment of the compensation agreed upon is a condition precedent to the separation.

[1] Hidaya.

[2] This is because three dirhams constitute the minimum dower; *cf. supra.*

III. Dissolution of Marriage by Judic a Decree

Apart from the dissolution of marriage by marital repudiation (*talak*) and by mutual consent (*khul'*), the law allows divorce by judicial decree, at the instance of either the wife or the husband. If the divorce is granted for some cause imputable to the husband, it is in effect a repudiation (*talak*). If, on the other hand, the cause is imputable to the wife, the divorce is described as an annulment (*faskh*). The practical difference is in the obligation to pay the dower and in the observance of the period of probation.

Dissolution by judicial decree, although a remedy for which either spouse may ask, is in practice usually sought by the wife rather than by the husband, since the husband has the absolute power to repudiate the wife without any cause stated. The grievances which entitle the wife to ask for a decree of separation may be considered under the following heads:

(1) Impotence.

(2) *Li'an,* or charging the wife with adultery.

(3) *Ila',* or making a vow to abstain from connection with the wife for at least four months.

(4) *Zihar,* or comparing the wife to any of the husband's female relatives within the prohibitive degrees.

(5) Failure to observe general marital obligations.

(6) Apostasy.

1. *Impotence.*

Impotence exists, in so far as the wife's claim for divorce is concerned, not only when the husband is physically incapable of connection with any woman, but also when he is unable to have intercourse with the complainant, that is, when he is impotent, as occidental lawyers say, *versus hanc.*

A wife may claim a judicial divorce on the ground of her husband's impotence at the time of the marriage, provided that she did not know of it, and that it has not since been removed. If she knew the husband to be impotent, she shall not be entitled "to have recourse to law for separation; just as a purchaser, who knew of a defect at the time of the sale, has no right to return the property purchased on account of the defect."[1]

If the husband admits impotency, the judge must grant a stay of judgment for a full year; "because that contains four seasons, and diseases are principally occasioned by an excess either of heat, cold, dryness or humidity, qualities which are peculiar to each season respectively; and it is probable that one of these four may particularly agree with the man's constitution, so as by its influence to dissipate his disease; thus it may be ascertained, when a year has completely elapsed, whether his inability proceeded from any radical infirmity, in which case it is impossible to retain the wife with humanity."[3]

When the period has expired, if the wife alleges continued non-intercourse and the husband denies the allegation, the judge is to appoint two women, to establish the fact by inspection of the wife. If the husband admits non-intercourse, or if the inspectors testify to the fact, the judge is to give the wife an option of divorce. If she maintains her demand for divorce, the judge will ask the husband to repudiate her; if he refuses to do so, the judge may pronounce a separation. Such a separation is an irrevocable divorce; and the wife is entitled to her whole dower, provided it be established that there has been, at any time, a valid "retirement." If the wife has declared

[1] Fet. Alemkiri, Vol. I, p. 707.
[2] Fet. Kazi Khan.
[3] Hidaya.

her option to maintain the marriage, she cannot then change her mind or make further complaint because of her husband's impotency. So if a man marries a woman but is not able to have intercourse with her, and the judge duly separates the two on account of the husband's impotency, and the man then marries her again—which he can well do, because the separation by the judge, as we have seen, amounts to one repudiation only—the woman shall have no option left to ask for a separation, because she had knowingly married an impotent man.[1]

If a marriage has been dissolved on other grounds than that of impotency, and if the parties remarry, the wife may demand a divorce on the ground that the husband is impotent; because it is to be assumed that the first marriage was consummated and that the wife had no reason to believe that the second marriage could not be.

If a woman has contracted marriage with a man from whom another woman has obtained a divorce on the ground of his impotence, and if the woman contracting the later marriage had knowledge of the cause of the separation, some hold that she cannot complain; but "the most correct doctrine is, that the second woman shall be entitled to have recourse to law, because a man is sometimes powerless with reference to one woman and not with reference to another."[2]

If the defect is in the person of the wife, there is a difference of opinion as to whether the contract may be annulled. All the Hanifite jurists are of opinion that a judicial separation may not be demanded by the husband for any cause whatsoever. Muhammed holds that if the wife is insane the contract may be annulled.[3] Shafi'ites, on the other hand, maintain that the contract may be an-

[1] Kazi Khan.
[2] Fet. Kazi Khan.
[3] Fet. Ali Effendi, p. 91.

nulled for any of the following five causes: leprosy, scrofula, madness, *ratk*[1] and *Karn.*[2] For recognition of the first of these causes, they find their authority in a tradition of the Prophet, who said: "Flee from lepers as ye would from a wild beast."

If annulment is to be granted on account of defect in the person of the wife, the man must be capable of intercourse. If there is incapacity on both sides, neither may complain of the other and the marriage will be upheld.[3]

2. *Li'an, or imprecation.*

When a husband charges his wife with adultery and the wife denies the charge, each supporting his or her assertion by invocation of divine wrath (*li'an*), the wife is entitled to a divorce.

Under the Muhammedan law a charge of adultery against a wife can be established only by the direct testimony of four witnesses. The historical reason for this stringent rule is interesting, in that it exemplifies the extent to which the legislation of Muhammed regarding matrimonial affairs was influenced by his family life and domestic troubles.

Muhammed, in 626, was returning from a successful expedition against the tribe of Bani Mustalik, followed by two of his wives, Ayesha and Umm Salma. One day Ayesha's litter was found to be empty and she herself was missing; but a few hours later one of Muhammed's adherents, Safwan, came into the city leading his camel with Ayesha seated thereon. The explanation given by Ayesha was that she had lost her necklace and had gone in search of it, and meanwhile the caravan had left. The Prophet at first seemed to regard the matter as suspicious, and a breach ensued, which was accentuated by the gossip

[1] *Vulva anteriore parte enascens.*
[2] Imperforate vagina.
[3] Fet. Kazi Khan.

of a certain other Muhammed. The scandal spread until Muhammed could no longer bear it, and he began to rebuke the slanderers of Ayesha publicly from the mosque pulpit. Later, becoming assured of the innocence of Ayesha, he fell into a trance, and on waking he wiped heavy drops of sweat from his brow and cried: "Rejoice, Ayesha! verily the Lord hath revealed thine innocence"; and Ayesha answered: "Praise be to God."

He then set out to punish the slanderers and to legislate against imputation of unchastity to women. It was on this occasion that the provision was revealed: "If any of your women be guilty of whoredom, produce four witnesses from amongst you against them. From the nature of the offence, the furnishing of ocular and direct evidence is almost always impossible. To obviate the evils which would necessarily result from a complete denial of redress, *li'an* was introduced.

It is an essential condition to divorce by *li'an* that the wife and the husband be competent to act as witnesses. Hence, a minor, or a person who is insane, impious, dumb, or blind, is not competent to take the *li'an*.

When unchastity is imputed to the wife, as by saying to her: "O! adultress!", she may prefer a complaint before the judge, demanding a *li'an*. *The* Fetawai Aelmkiri says that when the parties appear before the judge he should advise them to abandon the proceeding. Should they persist, the one in making the accusation, the other in demanding that the charge be proved, then the judge is to administer the prescribed oath, by which each invokes the curse of God if his or her assertion is untrue.[2] If the husband refuses to swear, the wife is granted a divorce. If not, he is first to repeat four times: "I attest by God, that I was a

[1] Mahmud Essad.
[2] Fet. Kazi Khan, p. 153.

speaker of the truth when I cast at her the charge of adultery," and after this he is to say: "The curse of God be upon me if I was a liar when I cast at her the charge of adultery." The wife is then to repeat four times: "I attest by God, that he is a liar in the charge of adultery that he has cast upon me," adding: "The wrath of God be upon me if he be a true speaker in the charge of adultery which he has cast upon me."[1]

After the imprecations are made, one view is that a separation takes place *ipso facto*. In support of this Zufer, a disciple of Hanifa, quotes the Prophet as having said: "The two who make imprecation can never come together," and, therefore, he holds that a perpetual prohibition of remarriage is established between them. Hanifa and his other disciples maintain, however, that the separation is not effected until the judge pronounces a decree of separation, which is treated as equivalent to a *talak bain*. According to this view, if after imprecation the husband acknowledges that his accusation was false, it is lawful for him to remarry the woman. Malikite and Shafi'ite schools uphold the opposite doctrine, namely, that a remarriage between the parties is perpetually prohibited.

Li'an proceedings may be instituted not only when the husband explicitly accuses his wife of adultery, but also when he impliedly imputes unchastity to her, as, for example, by denying that her child is his or that she is pregnant by him. The proceedings for *li'an* are the same in all cases, the only difference being that the formula is varied to suit the precise charge and its denial.

3. *Ila'*.

Ila' is abstinence from sexual intercourse for a period of not less than four months in the case of free women, and

[1] Hidaya.

not less than two months in the case of slaves, in pursuance of a vow to that effect.[1]

Before the Islamic legislation, "in times of ignorance,"[2] a vow of continence followed by an abstinence for a certain length of time was a method by which a man repudiated his wife. The principle was that the husband lost his right by non-user. No definite time limit seems to have been set prior to the Islamic legislation, and it is safe to presume that what determined was the intention of the husband to abandon his wife. The Prophet, seeing an injustice in constraining the wife to wait until the intention of the husband became apparent, set a time limit of four months,[3] during which period the husband is at liberty to break his vow and resume intercourse with his wife. The breaking of his vow may be expiated by manumitting a slave, feeding the poor, fasting for a number of days or similar good acts.[4] The Koran expressly permits this: "Those who swear off from their women, they must wait four months; but if they break their vow, God is forgiving and merciful."[5]

The husband may break his vow, normally, only by resuming matrimonial intercourse. Anything short of that, such as kissing, touching or "looking at her nakedness with desire"[6] is not sufficient. But if he be sick and incapable of intercourse, or if his wife be temporarily incapacitated, he may nullify the effect of the oath by a declaration to that effect, as, for example, by saying: "I have returned to that woman,"[7] upon which *ila'* ceases. Shafi'i, however, is of the

[1] Fet. Ali Effendi, p. 100.
[2] Hidaya. Muhammedan writers always refer to the time before the establishment of Muhammedanism as the "times of ignorance."
[3] Hidaya.
[4] Koran, Ch. II, v. 226.
[5] Inaya, Vol. II, p. 218.
[6] Hidaya.

opinion that nothing short of matrimonial intercourse is sufficient to cancel an *ali'*.

After the lapse of the period, the husband loses his conjugal rights over the wife, who becomes entitled to claim a dissolution of marriage by the judge.

The Hanifite jurists contend that an irreversible divorce takes place independent of any decree of separation by the magistrate.[1] Shafi'i and Malik,[2] on the other hand, maintain that a decree of the magistrate is requisite, "because the husband here withholds her right from his wife, and hence the magistrate acts as his substitute in effecting a separation; as in the case of eunuchs and impotent persons . . . separation rests with the woman."[3]

There is a difference of opinion also as to who are competent to pronounce an *ila'*; Abu Hanifa holding that those are competent to pronounce an *ila'* who may effect a valid repudiation, while his two disciples maintain that only those on whom expiation is incumbent are capable of pronouncing it.[4]

The words may, as in other instances, be either express (*sarih*), as: "By God, I will not approach thee," "I will not lie with thee," or they may be ambiguous, metaphorical (*kinayah*), as "Her head shall not be joined to mine." *Ila'* may be effected not only by swearing to God, but also by a vow, together with a pledge of pilgrimage, fast or almsgiving in case the vow be broken.

4. *Zihar.*

Literally, *zihar* means the back; in law it means that a husband has compared his wife to any of his female rela-

[1] Hidaya.
[2] Ibn Abu Zayd.
[3] Hidaya. Clavel, Droit Musulman, Vol. I, p. 245.
[4] Expiation is incumbent on persons who are legally capable of making a vow. Minors, insane persons, *etc.*, are incaable of making a vow.

tives within the prohibitive degrees.

The ancient Arabs sometimes divorced their wives by the words: "You are to me like the back (*zahr*) of my mother." The husband then in all respects regarded his wife as his mother, and she became related to his kindred in the same degree as if she were really so. A woman divorced in this manner could not marry again under any circumstance.

Hidaya speaks of this method of divorce as established in the "times of ignorance." The Islamic law treats such a declaration by the husband as equivalent to a vow of continence (*zihar*), which binds him until the performance of expiation, and which, if maintained, gives the wife a claim for judicial separation.

It is not quite clear whether the comparisons in question were regarded by the ancient Arabs as *"assimilations injurieuses,"*[1] or as promoting the woman from the subordinate status of a wife to the highly honorable position of an adoptive mother.[2] It is probable that each view was held, but at different historic periods. Whatever may have been its original significance, there is no doubt that, at the time of Muhammed, this mode of divorce, as Amir Ali says, had become so frequent and had assumed so mischievous a character, that it tended to degrade the morality of the Arab tribes beyond any other custom.[3]

To put an end to it Muhammed said: "God hath not given a man two hearts within him; neither hath he made your wives (some of whom ye divorce, regarding them thereafter as your mothers) your true mothers"[4]; and "As to those among you who divorce their wives, by declaring that they will thereafter regard them as their mothers, let

[1] Sautayra et Cherbonneau, Droit Musulman, Vol. I, p. 314.
[2] Robertson Smith, Marriage and Kinship in Early Arabia, p. 389.
[3] Syed Ameer Ali, Mahommedan Law, Vol. II, p. 456.
[4] Koran, Ch. XXXIII, v. 4.

them know that they are not their mothers. They only are their mothers who brought them forth, and they certainly utter an unjustifiable saying and a falsehood." [1] At the same time, the use of language which was considered as an outrage on public morals was checked by giving the wife a right to ask for a dissolution of the marriage tie by a judicial decree, unless the husband expiate the sin in the prescribed manner. The wife was permitted to refuse herself to him until he had performed the penance prescribed by law for such cases, and to apply to the court for an order requiring him to perform the penance or to give her a regular divorce such as would entitle her to deferred dower and enable her to marry another.

To enable her to do this, however, it is essential that the comparison be applied either to the whole body or to such of its parts as are improper to be seen. Hence, if a husband says: "Your head to me is like the head of my mother," *zihar* is not established.[2] But if he says "You are to me like the belly, or thigh, of my mother," *zihar* is established.[3]

It is also a condition of *zihar* that the husband be a person capable of making expiation, the *zihar* of a non-Muhammedan, a minor or an insane person being of no effect. It is, however, not necessary that the comparison be made in earnest: *zihar* made in jest, under duress, or by mistake is valid. Expiation of a *zihar* is effected by an emancipation of a slave, by a fast of two months, or by feeding the poor.

The circumstances under which this rule was established are interesting. Sautayra[4] relates the story of a woman named Kaula bint Talaha, who was divorced by her husband, Aus Ibn Es-Sauat, in this manner, *i. e.*, by *zihar*. The divorced woman thereupon called upon the Prophet

[1] Koran, Ch. LVIII, v. 2.
[2] Fet. Feizié, p. 150.
[3] Hidaya.
[4] Droit Musulman, Vol. I, p. 314.

and complained that a permanent separation would involve hardship for both the husband and the wife, as they had children to care for. Muhammed, being touched by this plea, retired and came out with a revelation on the subject. "Those who divorce their wives by declaring that they will for the future regard them as their mothers, and afterwards would repair what they have said, shall be obliged to free a captive before they touch one another. That is what ye are warned to perform . . . and who find not a captive to redeem shall observe a fast of two consecutive months, before they shall touch one another. And those who shall not be able to fast during so long a time, shall feed three score poor men."[1] Malikites say: "It is more commendable according to our view to pray and fast."[2]

To sum up: *zihar* does not invalidate the marriage *ipso facto*. It merely renders matrimonial intercourse unlawful, until the comparison is withdrawn and expiation is made. If the man has connection with his wife before he makes expiation, he is not guilty of fornication; but "it behooves him to repent and pray forgiveness from God; but nothing is incumbent upon him except the expiation on account of *zihar*, as before, and that he refrain from any repetition of the carnal act with her until he perform such expiation."[3] If the *zihar* is not withdrawn, then the judge may grant the wife a divorce.

5. *Failure to discharge general marital obligations.*

When the husband acts in such a way as to make matrimonial life intolerable to his wife, as by neglecting to perform duties imposed upon him by law or by failing to fulfill engagements voluntarily entered into, the wife has a right to sue the husband for a decree of divorce.[4] This power

[1] Koran, Ch. LVIII, v. 3 and 4.
[2] Ibn Abu Zayd.
[3] Hidaya.
[4] The duties of the husband are set forth *supra*, in Part II of this essay.

the judge has derived from the sayings of the Prophet, to the effect that "if marriage caused prejudice to a woman, let it be broken off."[1]

During his own lifetime Muhammed had occasion to apply this rule in a notable instance, which furnished an authoritative precedent for the Muhammedan jurists. Sautayra[2] relates the story. A woman named Sabia Bint Haris, married to a man called Amr, took refuge in a Muhammedan camp. Her husband was asked to follow her, but refused to do so. The marriage was annulled and Sabia was declared free to contract a new marriage.

Although the Arabic sources assert in general terms the right of the wife to claim a divorce if the husband fails to fulfill the terms of the marriage contract or to perform the obligations imposed on him by law, I have been unable to find specific cases in which divorce has been granted for such causes. In their statement of the theory, the Malikites are perhaps more explicit than the writers of the other three schools. The Hanifites are silent on the subject; but in the writings of the Malikite jurists and of their commentators there are statements that the Hanifites have interpreted this right of the wife more strictly than the Malikites and have in many instances denied divorce to the wife where the Malikites have freely granted it.[3]

Sautayra[4] cites a number of cases in which divorce has been granted because of the husband's conduct. Among the principal causes recognized in these decisions are the following:

(1) When the husband leaves the wife without means of subsistence.

(2) When he deprives the wife of raiment.

(3) When he forces her to beg for her living.

[1] Bukhari.
[2] Statut Personnel, Vol. I, p. 253.
[3] Nores, Essai de Codification du droit Musulman, p. 233.
[4] Sautayra, Droit Musulman, Vol. 1, p. 354, *et seq.*

(4) When he refuses to provide a habitation for her.

(5) When he leaves the conjugal domicile without making any provision on her behalf.

(6) When he abandons her and refuses to visit her.

(7) When he treats her cruelly.

(8) When he beats her without cause.

(9) When he tries to introduce a concubine into the conjugal domicile.[1]

There is a difference of opinion as to the condition under which a wife is entitled to claim a divorce for non-maintenance. According to the Hanifites, inability to provide maintenance is not a sufficient ground for asking a divorce. When the husband is possessed of means and is able to provide for the support of both himself and his wife, and wilfully refuses to do so and neglects her, then only can she apply for a divorce. The judge has the power of granting a divorce, when the refusal or neglect is wilful and unjustifiable. But if the husband be indigent and has niether the means to provide for her support nor ability to work, she cannot obtain a separation as a matter of right. Under the Shafi'ite law, however, inability to provide maintenance, wilful or otherwise, is a cause for which the judge (*kadi*) may dissolve the marriage.[2]

The Malikites hold not only that the husband is obliged to maintain his wife, but that he must provide her with maintenance according to the standard of living to which she was accustomed before she was married.[3]

Refusal to support must be persistent. No divorce may be granted for non-support if the husband shows willingness to make proper provision and the judge is satisfied that the offense will not be repeated. In such instances the judge is authorized to use his discretion. If the husband abandons

[1] Nores, Essai de codification du droit Musulman, p. 254.
[2] Syed Ameer Ali, Vol. II, p. 451.
[3] Sidi Khalil and Sautayra.

the conjugal domicile and leaves his wife without means of support, she has a right to apply to the judge, who is authorized to adjourn the case for thirty days.[1] If the husband fails to appear during this period, the judge may pronounce a decree of divorce.

Unequal treatment of wives is another ground for granting a divorce to the wife who is prejudiced. "If the husband does not live with one wife for a month and she has recourse to the judge (*kadi*), complaining that the husband is not living with her, the judge shall direct the husband to observe equality between his wives in future; and if he fails to do this, the judge shall inflict punishment, in consequence of the husband having failed to observe equality notwithstanding the injunction."[2] In 1865 the Court of Algiers held that when a man upon his second marriage ceased to have any matrimonial relations with his first wife, the latter was entitled to a decree of divorce.[3] It is highly improbable, however, that the Hanifites would consider this as a valid ground for divorce.

Modern jurists have granted divorce to women in cases in which divorce might have been denied under the older Muhammedan rules. For example, Sautayra cites a case decided by the highest Algerian Court, in which a woman sued her husband for separation on the ground of cruelty. The court held that it was no defense to a claim for divorce on the ground of cruelty, that the cruelty was the result of the wife's own conduct. In this case it appeared that the man beat his wife because she blasphemed the Musulman religion. It is improbable that such a decision would have been rendered in the earlier days. The law expressly confers on a husband "the power of correction,"[4] and correcting a blasphemous wife would not only be within his

[1] Sautayra, p. 256.
[2] Kazi Khan.
[3] Sautayra, Droit Musulman, p. 258.
[4] Hidaya.

right, but would probably be considered to be his duty.

It may be observed that the liberal interpretation of this branch of the law by the Malikites is largely due to the influence of the French in northwestern Africa, who with remarkable wisdom have utilized the indigenous institutions to alleviate the position of the Muhammedan women. With characteristic ingenuity, out of a mass of uncertain primitive traditions they have developed a system of law which can sustain a comparison with some of the most modern European legislations. In doing this, they have not only realized the ideal aimed at by marriage in the Muhammedan law, but they have also furnished an example of the lawmaking power of interpretation.

6. *Apostasy.*

Abandonment of the Muhammedan faith by either of the spouses is a cancellation of their marriage, which takes effect *ipso facto.* In this case there is no need for a judicial decree.[1] Strictly speaking, the marriage is perhaps suspended rather than annulled, since it becomes valid again *ipso facto,* if the apostate be reconverted to Islam. As soon as the apostate returns to Islam, he may resume the marital tie without entering into a new marriage contract.

If both husband and wife abjure the faith of Islam at the same time, their marriage is by a "favorable construction of the law permitted to endure."[2] Zufer disagrees from this view; "but our doctors (Hanifites), in support of their opinion, cite an instance recorded to have happened in the time of the blessed companions (of the Prophet), when the tribe of Bani Hanifa, after having apostatized, returned to the faith, and the companions did not direct them to renew their marriages."[3] But this decision would

[1] Durr-al-Mukhtar, p. 216.

[2] Hidaya.

[3] Ibid.

have been reached under either theory.

Conversion to the Islamic faith on the part of the man, where both parties previously professed one of the revealed religions (Christianity or Judaism) does not impair the matrimonial relation, even though the wife retains her non-Muhammedan religion; but if the husband was an idolater and was married to a woman of the same faith, the union is dissolved by the husband's conversion to Muhammedanism unless the wife also accepts it. If a Christian or Jewish woman, married to a man of the same faith, becomes a Muhammedan, the marriage is dissolved unless the husband also adopts Muhammedanism.

Bei Fragen zur Produktsicherheit wenden Sie sich bitte an:
If you have any questions regarding product safety,
please contact:

Walter de Gruyter GmbH
Genthiner Straße 13
10785 Berlin
productsafety@degruyterbrill.com